OPERATION
COBRA

The 'Battle Zone Normandy' Series

All of these titles can be ordered via the
Sutton Publishing website
www.suttonpublishing.co.uk

**The 'Battle Zone Normandy'
Editorial and Design Team**

Series Editor Simon Trew

Senior Commissioning Editor Jonathan Falconer

Assistant Editor Nick Reynolds

Cover and Page Design Martin Latham

Editing and Layout Donald Sommerville

Mapping Map Creation Ltd

Photograph Scanning and Mapping Bow Watkinson

Index Michael Forder

BATTLE
ZONE
NORMANDY

OPERATION
COBRA

CHRISTOPHER PUGSLEY

Series Editor: Simon Trew

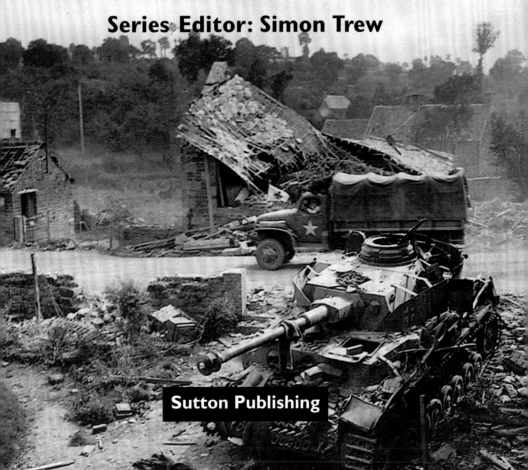

Sutton Publishing

First Published in 2004 by
Sutton Publishing Limited · Phoenix Mill
Thrupp · Stroud · Gloucestershire · GL5 2BU

Text Copyright © Christopher Pugsley 2004
Tour map overlays Copyright © Sutton
   Publishing
Tour base maps Copyright © Institut
   Géographique National, Paris
GSGS (1944) map overlays Copyright ©
   Sutton Publishing
GSGS (1944) base maps Copyright ©
   The British Library/Crown Copyright

Christopher Pugsley has asserted the moral
right to be identified as the author of this work.

British Library Cataloguing in Publication Data
A catalogue record for this book is available
from The British Library.

ISBN 0-7509-3015-2

While every effort has been made to ensure
that the information given in this book is
accurate, the publishers, the author and the
series editor do not accept responsibility for
any errors or omissions or for any changes in
the details given in this guide or for the
consequence of any reliance on the
information provided. The publishers would be
grateful if readers would advise them of any
inaccuracies they may encounter so these can
be considered for future editions of this book.
The inclusion of any place to stay, place to eat,
tourist attraction or other establishment in
this book does not imply an endorsement or
recommendation by the publisher, the series
editor or the author. Their details are included
for information only. Directions are for
guidance only and should be used in
conjunction with other sources of information.

Pugsley, Christ...

Operation Cobra
/ Christopher
Pugsley

British Library Cataloguing in Publication Data
This book is available

1591971

940.
5421

Typeset in 10.5/14 pt Sabon

...ound in England by
... Co. Ltd, Sparkford

Front cover: US M5 Stuart light tanks pass through Coutances, 30 July 1944. (United States National Archives [USNA])

Page 1: Monument in Périers to the 'Tough Ombres' of 90th US Infantry Division. A fourth figure has since been added to complete the monument. (Author)

Page 3: Supply trucks roll through Pont-Farcy on the road to Vire on 5 August past a knocked-out Panzer IV of 3rd Panzer Regiment, 2nd Panzer Division. (USNA)

Page 7: Checking out a destroyed Sturmgeschütz III assault gun, Marigny, 29 July 1944. (USNA)

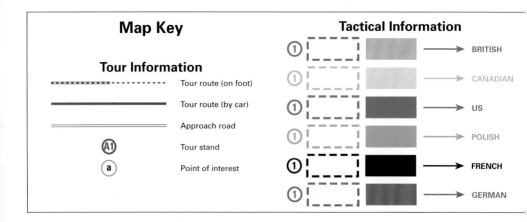

Map Key

Tour Information

·········· - - - - -	Tour route (on foot)
▬▬▬▬▬	Tour route (by car)
═════════	Approach road
(A1)	Tour stand
(a)	Point of interest

Tactical Information

① ⬚	▬▬ →	BRITISH
① ⬚	▬▬ →	CANADIAN
① ⬚	▬▬ →	US
① ⬚	▬▬ →	POLISH
① ⬛	▬▬ →	FRENCH
① ⬚	▬▬ →	GERMAN

CONTENTS

THE NORMANDY BATTLEFIELD, 24 JULY 1944

Legend:

Allied front line, evening 24 July

VII CORPS US formation
I CORPS Canadian formation
XII CORPS British formation
I SS CORPS German formation

xxx Corps boundary
xxxx Army boundary

Contour 50 metres
Contour 100 metres
Contour 200 metres
Inundated area

Kilometres
0 10 20

CABOURG

CAP DE LA HAGUE

Auderville

Beaumont-Hague

CHERBOURG

CAP LÉVI

St-Pierre-Église

Barfleur

POINTE DE BARFLEUR

Tourlaville

Quettehou

Delasse

St-Vaast-la-Hougue

Quinéville

VALOGNES

Montebourg

R. Merderet

Ste-Mère-Église

Pont-l'Abbé

Chef-du-Pont

Bricquebec

Barneville

St-Sauveur-le-Vicomte

R. Douve

Orglandes

St-Sauveur-Lendelin

les Pieux

CAP DE CARTERET

St-Lô-d'Ourville

la Haye-du-Puits

CAP DE FLAMANVILLE

Lessay

Périers

R. Taute

FIRST US ARMY

VIII CORPS

LXXXIV CORPS

St-Sauveur-Lendelin

COUTANCES

Marigny

SEVENTH ARMY

Condé-sur-Vire

II PARA CORPS

St-Lô

XIX CORPS

Pont-Hébert

Villiers-Fossard

St-Jean-de-Daye

VII CORPS

Carentan

Montmartin-en-Graignes

Isigny

Grandcamp-les-Bains

Vierville-sur-Mer

Bérigny

St-Clair-sur-l'Elle

V CORPS

Balleroy

Trungy

R. Drôme

Caumont

Noyers-Bocage

XXX CORPS

Hottot-les-Bagues

Villers-Bocage

Tilly-sur-Seulles

XII CORPS

Évrecy

R. Odon

St-Manvieu

Carpiquet

CAEN

II CAN CORPS

I CAN CORPS

FIRST CANADIAN ARMY

I CORPS

May-sur-Orne

Cagny

Vimont

I SS CORPS

R. Dives

Troarn

Hérouvillette

LXXXVI CORPS

Cabourg

Ouistreham

Lion-sur-Mer

Cambes

Courseulles-sur-Mer

R. Seulles

VIII CORPS

BAYEUX

Port-en-Bessin

R. Aure

le Molay-Littry

R. Drôme

Arromanches-les-Bains

SECOND (BRITISH) ARMY

Bay of the Seine

PART ONE
INTRODUCTION

BATTLE ZONE NORMANDY

The Battle of Normandy was one of the greatest military clashes of all time. From late 1943, when the Allies appointed their senior commanders and began the air operations that were such a vital preliminary to the invasion, until the end of August 1944, it pitted against one another several of the most powerful nations on earth, as well as some of their most brilliant minds. When it was won, it changed the world forever. The price was high, but for anybody who values the principles of freedom and democracy, it is difficult to conclude that it was one not worth paying.

I first visited Lower Normandy in 1994, a year after I joined the War Studies Department at the Royal Military Academy Sandhurst (RMAS). With the 50th anniversary of D-Day looming, it was decided that the British Army would be represented at several major ceremonies by one of the RMAS's officer cadet companies. It was also suggested that the cadets should visit some of the battlefields, not least to bring home to them the significance of why they were there. Thus, at the start of June 1994, I found myself as one of a small team of military and civilian directing staff flying with the cadets in a draughty and noisy Hercules transport to visit the beaches and fields of Calvados, in my case for the first time.

I was hooked. Having met some of the veterans and seen the ground over which they fought – and where many of their friends died – I was determined to go back. Fortunately, the Army encourages battlefield touring as part of its soldiers' education, and on numerous occasions since 1994 I have been privileged to return to Normandy, often to visit new sites. In the process I have learned a vast amount, both from my colleagues (several of whom are contributors to this series) and from my enthusiastic and sometimes tri-service audiences, whose professional insights and penetrating questions have frequently made me re-examine my own assumptions and prejudices. Perhaps inevitably, especially when standing in one of Normandy's beautifully-maintained Commonwealth War Graves Commission cemeteries, I have also found myself deeply moved by the critical events that took place there in the summer of 1944.

'Battle Zone Normandy' was conceived by Jonathan Falconer, Commissioning Editor at Sutton Publishing, in 2001. Why not, he suggested, bring together recent academic research – some of which challenges the general perception of what happened on and after 6 June 1944 – with a perspective based on familiarity with the ground itself? We agreed that the opportunity existed for a series that would set out to combine detailed and accurate narratives, based mostly on primary sources, with illustrated guides to the ground itself, which could be used either in the field (sometimes quite literally), or by the armchair explorer. The book in your hands is the product of that agreement.

The 'Battle Zone Normandy' series consists of 14 volumes, covering most of the major and many of the minor engagements that went together to create the Battle of Normandy. The first six books deal with the airborne and amphibious landings on 6 June 1944, and with the struggle to create the firm lodgement that was the prerequisite for eventual Allied victory. Five further volumes cover some of the critical battles that followed, as the Allies' plans unravelled and they were forced to improvise a battle very different from that originally intended. Finally, the last three titles in the series examine the fruits of the bitter attritional struggle of June and July 1944, as the Allies irrupted through the German lines or drove them back in fierce fighting. The series ends, logically enough, with the devastation of the German armed forces in the 'Falaise Pocket' in late August.

Whether you use these books while visiting Normandy, or to experience the battlefields vicariously, we hope you will find them as interesting to read as we did to research and write. Far from the inevitable victory that is sometimes represented, D-Day and the ensuing battles were full of hazards and unpredictability. Contrary to the view often expressed, had the invasion failed, it is far from certain that a second attempt could have been mounted. Remember this, and the significance of the contents of this book, not least for your life today, will be the more obvious.

Dr Simon Trew
Royal Military Academy Sandhurst
December 2003

INTRODUCTION

ACKNOWLEDGEMENTS

Researching and writing 'Battle Zone Normandy', *Operation Cobra* has been a delight. It opened my eyes to American achievements in Normandy and has given me examples at company and battalion level that I wish I had been aware of 23 years ago when instructing at Tactical School in New Zealand.

I thank Dr Simon Trew, my colleague in the Department of War Studies at the Royal Military Academy Sandhurst for inviting me to be part of the writing team under his dedicated editorship of the series. I am also appreciative of the meticulous care both he and Bow Watkinson showed in the preparation of maps for this volume. This care and attention to detail has also been the hallmark of Jonathan Falconer and Nick Reynolds and their team at Sutton Publishing and they have my thanks. Donald Sommerville has been the consummate editor in reducing the massive draft I produced to him into a balanced text yet doing so in a way that retained my words and my way of saying things for which I am grateful. Andrew Orgill and his staff at the Central Library, RMA Sandhurst, as always, anticipated the books I needed and confirmed once again the pleasure of researching at Sandhurst. As always I cannot fault the advice and assistance I have received, and any mistakes or omissions are my own.

In the USA my friend Dr Gordon Rudd offered insights into American doctrine and their way of doing military business and with Sevgi provided a home base on my weekend breaks from research. Timothy Nenninger and Mitch Yokelson at the National Archives were friendliness itself and they and their staffs went out of their way to provide advice and assistance during my research trips to Washington, with Mitch providing transport and local knowledge as escort to some superb second-hand bookshops.

'Rhino' tank conversions, to allow vehicles to pass through Normandy's hedgerows, were a US secret weapon for Operation Cobra. *Top right:* A Rhino-equipped Stuart tank beside a hedgerow it has breached. *Right:* Two views of Rhinos being constructed from former German beach defences. (USNA)

My wife Dee has put up with the strains of yet another deadline and willingly spent two summer holidays touring Normandy while I walked the ground. As always I am thankful to her and our children, Joanna, Susan, and David, and our grandson Dylan for continuing to put up with an obsessive historian in the family and they all have my love.

The monument to Operation Cobra, Generals Bradley and Collins, and to the 'Glorieux Combattants du VII Corps U.S.', located at the junction of the D900 and the road to la Chapelle-en-Juger, the D189. *(Author)*

DEDICATION

This book is dedicated to three people.

To my father-in-law, Raymond Dean Osborne, Staff Sergeant, Transportation Corps, US Army, who left El Dorado Springs, Missouri to go to war and served in the Southwest Pacific. He met and married a Sydney girl, and made Australia his home.

To my mother, Olwen Jones, (1922–2004) who joined the ATS in 1939 and served as a driver in the United Kingdom until demobilised in 1945, and to my father, Francis William Pugsley, who sailed as an apprentice deck officer in the Merchant Service with the Anglo-Iranian Oil Company on the *British Splendour* on the Atlantic run for eight months in 1940–1 and then, after being invalided out, served as a private in the Penarth Home Guard.

Christopher Pugsley
Department of War Studies, RMA Sandhurst

PART TWO

HISTORY

CHAPTER I

BACKGROUND TO COBRA

This book is the story of Operation 'Cobra', the critical battle that led to the break-out of American forces from the Cotentin Peninsula, Allied success in Normandy and the collapse of the German forces in France. It turned what had been a battle of attrition in Normandy throughout late June and July 1944 into a war of movement and heralded the coming of age of the United States ground forces in the Second World War. It demonstrated how much had been learned by the American forces in the period between the landings on D-Day, 6 June, and the beginning of Operation Cobra on 25 July, seven weeks later.

Above: Périers' Place Général Leclerc, a critical road junction leading south to Coutances and east to St-Lô. A *Cobra – la Percée* ('Cobra – the Break-Through') roadside sign tells the story of the town during the summer of 1944. These signs can be found at all major sites and give an invaluable insight into the civilian experience during the Battle of Normandy. *(Author)*

Page 13: An M8 Greyhound armoured car passing the church and war memorial in the destroyed village of la Chapelle-en-Juger, 27 July. *(USNA)*

Cobra involved the concentration of Lieutenant General (Lt Gen) Omar N. Bradley's First US Army, numbering 15 divisions, with a further four earmarked for Lt Gen George S. Patton's Third US Army in reserve. These forces were concentrated on the right flank of the Allied bridgehead across the neck of the Cotentin Peninsula. In particular VIII and VII US Corps took position along the line of the Lessay–Périers–St-Lô road. Securing this had taken weeks of hard fighting in country ideal for defence. By the first days of August two American armies, First and Third, were in being and the stage was set for the defeat of German forces in France.

THE STRATEGIC SITUATION

Throughout June and July 1944 General Dwight D. Eisenhower, Supreme Commander, Allied Expeditionary Force, oversaw the fighting from his Supreme Headquarters Allied Expeditionary Force in England. Although Eisenhower would establish a tactical headquarters in France in July, operational control of the ground battle remained with General Sir Bernard L. Montgomery. As commander of 21st Army Group, Montgomery directed two armies, Second (British) Army and First US Army.

Eisenhower and Montgomery, 26 July 1944. (USNA)

Two further armies were being assembled in France: First Canadian Army, which would become part of Montgomery's 21st Army Group; and Third US Army. At Cobra's end the American forces in Europe would be reorganised as 12th Army Group under Bradley's command, including Third Army and with Lt Gen Courtney H. Hodges assuming command of First Army.

Since the D-Day landings on 6 June 1944 the bridgehead had been consolidated, the Cotentin Peninsula isolated and the port of Cherbourg captured. British attempts to expand the eastern perimeter or left flank of the Allied forces around Caen had not been as successful; despite a series of offensives, Caen was not completely captured until 18 July. This failure to meet pre-D-Day

HISTORY

planning targets had led to growing tensions, exacerbated by the personalities of the key commanders. In particular, members of Eisenhower's staff were critical of Montgomery's performance. However, the intensity of the fighting on Second (British) Army's front facing Panzer Group West had helped to draw in the bulk of the German armour. By contrast, the American forces on the west or right flank of the Allied position faced the resource-starved German Seventh Army, although this was operating in what was seen as ideal defensive terrain.

Operation Cobra grew out of Bradley's proposal to break Seventh Army's defensive crust by mounting an offensive supported by a massive air strike, with the aim of gaining ground for manoeuvre and moving on the Brittany ports, identified as vital to the build-up of American forces on the continent. While Montgomery remained overall ground commander, Operation Cobra was very much Bradley's brain-child and its course and conduct his battle.

An M8 Howitzer Motor Carriage leads vehicles of 3rd Armored Division through Montreuil-sur-Lozon on the road to Marigny, 26 July. *(USNA)*

THE GROUND

By late July the Allied front in Normandy consisted of the British and Canadian forces on the left or eastern flank around Caen and the Americans on the right or western flank across the neck of the Cotentin Peninsula. The British were attempting to advance south of Caen over the dry windswept limestone plains north of Falaise,

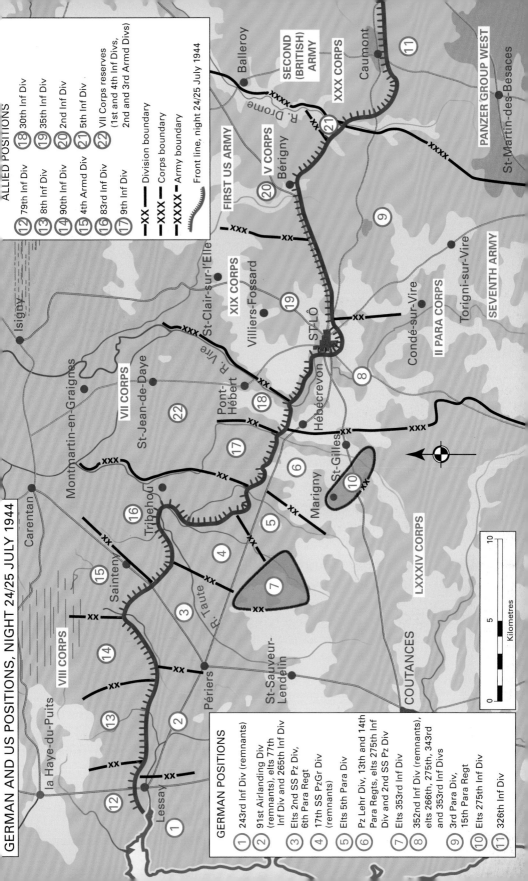

GERMAN AND US POSITIONS, NIGHT 24/25 JULY 1944

ALLIED POSITIONS

- ⑫ 79th Inf Div
- ⑬ 8th Inf Div
- ⑭ 90th Inf Div
- ⑮ 4th Armd Div
- ⑯ 83rd Inf Div
- ⑰ 9th Inf Div
- ⑱ 30th Inf Div
- ⑲ 35th Inf Div
- ⑳ 2nd Inf Div
- ㉑ 5th Inf Div
- ㉒ VII Corps reserves (1st and 4th Inf Divs, 2nd and 3rd Armd Divs)

— **xx** — Division boundary
— **xxx** — Corps boundary
— **xxxx** — Army boundary
〰〰〰 Front line, night 24/25 July 1944

GERMAN POSITIONS

- ① 243rd Inf Div (remnants)
- ② 91st Airlanding Div (remnants), elts 77th Inf Div and 265th Inf Div
- ③ Elts 2nd SS Pz Div, 6th Para Regt
- ④ 17th SS PzGr Div (remnants)
- ⑤ Elts 5th Para Div
- ⑥ Pz Lehr Div, 13th and 14th Para Regts, elts 275th Inf Div and 2nd SS Pz Div
- ⑦ Elts 353rd Inf Div
- ⑧ 352nd Inf Div (remnants), elts 266th, 275th, 343rd and 353rd Inf Divs
- ⑨ 3rd Para Div, 15th Para Regt
- ⑩ Elts 275th Inf Div
- ⑪ 326th Inf Div

SECOND (BRITISH) ARMY
XXX CORPS
PANZER GROUP WEST
FIRST US ARMY
V CORPS
XIX CORPS
VII CORPS
VIII CORPS
SEVENTH ARMY
II PARA CORPS
LXXXIV CORPS
COUTANCES

Balleroy
Caumont
St-Martin-des-Besaces
R. Drôme
Bérigny
St-Clair-sur-l'Elle
Villiers-Fossard
ST-LÔ
Condé-sur-Vire
Torigni-sur-Vire
Isigny
Carentan
Montmartin-en-Graignes
St-Jean-de-Daye
Pont-Hébert
Hébécrevon
Marigny
St-Gilles
Tribehou
Sainteny
Lessay
la Haye-du-Puits
Périers
St-Sauveur-Lendelin
R. Vire
R. Taute

Kilometres
0   5   10

The thick hedgerows of the *bocage* provided natural fortifications for the defender. Here a 60-mm mortar crew keeps up a steady fire from a covered position in a typical lane while infantry manoeuvre forward. *(USNA)*

traditionally farmed for wheat and cattle with few enclosures and better suited to armoured operations. Their failure to achieve this shifted the emphasis to the centre and western sectors of the front.

The centre and right flank of the Allied front presented very different terrain to the attacker. In the centre, between the Rivers Orne and Vire, was a maze of hilly country that increased in height and complexity as one proceeded south, forming a mass of low ridges divided by narrow valleys, ideal for defence.

West of the Vire were the Normandy woodlands or *bocage,* covering chalk lands fissured by a network of streams, which over the centuries had encouraged intensive farming methods. The area was typified by small fields enclosed by hedgerows grown on earthen banks, forming a maze of narrow sunken roads and tracks edged by high hedges. These were traditionally neatly trimmed annually up to a loaded cart's height, so that above this the branches would resemble waves of green rolling in from either side of the road, which would sometimes form claustrophobic archways over those passing beneath. The hedges, sometimes as thick and tough as fortress walls, enclosed fields, meadows and orchards across country where distinct ridges running north–south were interspersed with river meadows and large open areas of marshy land.

Once it was evident that they could not throw the invaders back into the sea, the German defenders used the characteristics of the land to best advantage. They destroyed the sluice gates that regulated the tidal influence on the river levels, flooding the river flats and marshes of the *prairies marécageuses*, creating corridors of land along the ridge lines that channelled the attackers' movements, forcing them to advance along narrow isthmuses against defence that made best use of the hedgerows of the *bocage*. The centuries-old hedges bordering each field and narrow cart-width lane negated the Allied advantage in tank numbers and provided ideal cover and killing areas for a skilled defender to use.

CHAPTER 2

THE GERMAN FORCES

Hitler's Third Reich was under pressure on all fronts. In the east the series of Red Army offensives had shattered the German defences, leading to the advance of the Red Army into Poland and towards the Balkans. In Italy the Gustav Line had been breached and then Rome had fallen in June. Attempts to throw the Normandy invaders back into the sea had failed. Now the *Wehrmacht* (German armed forces) could only hold on and look to their *Führer* to produce a miracle. Sustaining a defensive line was the key to this strategy and the Normandy terrain allowed overstretched German resources the best options in maintaining a defensive front in France.

The failure of the assassination attempt against Hitler on 20 July 1944 deepened the *Führer*'s distrust of his generals and consolidated his absolute rule of the Third Reich. The success of Panzer Group West in stopping Operation 'Goodwood', the British and Canadian drive to the south-east of Caen between 18 and 20 July, convinced him that Seventh Army facing the Americans could successfully employ the same approach. Accordingly, *Starre Verteidigung* ('stand fast') was the order of the day. There was no strategic concept in place, only holding on, and nothing to fall back on should it fail.

HISTORY

Hitler and his generals saw the British operations around Caen as the greatest threat and this area became the point of main effort in the German defensive plan. The bulk of the German forces in Normandy were concentrated against Second (British) Army on the eastern flank, where the more open ground was more suitable for mass armoured operations. Here was grouped the bulk of the German armour under the control of Panzer Group West, which was formed as a separate command from Seventh Army.

Generalfeldmarschall (Field Marshal) Hans-Günther von Kluge had replaced Field Marshal Gerd von Rundstedt as Commander-in-Chief, West in early July. Only Field Marshal Erwin Rommel, commanding Army Group B, survived of the senior German D-Day commanders and he, too, would disappear from the scene when wounded in a Spitfire attack on 17 July, with Kluge assuming direct command of Army Group B in his place. The outstanding armoured commander *General der Panzertruppen* (General of Armoured Troops) Heinrich Eberbach now commanded Panzer Group West and the 64-year-old *SS-Oberstgruppenführer* (General) Paul Hausser was promoted from II SS Panzer Corps to assume command of Seventh Army after his predecessor, *Generaloberst* (Colonel-General) Friedrich Dollmann, killed himself on 28 June.

Hausser was a veteran in every sense; he had won the Iron Cross in the First World War and retired as a professional soldier in the rank of *Generalleutnant* (GenLt) in 1932. A staunch supporter of the Nazi Party, he became involved in the formation of the *Waffen-SS* (the Nazi Party's own armed forces), and had earned the title of the 'father of the *Waffen-SS*'. Despite his operational experience on the Eastern Front, both Kluge and Rommel saw Hausser as a political general and were reluctant to have him promoted to army command, but were overruled by Hitler.

Seventh Army consisted of two corps. LXXXIV Corps held the western sector from the coast at Lessay almost to the River Vire. It was commanded by GenLt Dietrich von Choltitz, a highly experienced officer who had won the Knight's Cross as a battalion commander during the campaign in France in 1940 and who was posted to Normandy in June 1944 from a corps command on the Italian front. II Paratroop Corps held the eastern sector on the Vire around St-Lô, with the inter-corps boundary being along the line Hébécrevon–St-Gilles. This weak corps of two divisions was led by a First World War artillery veteran, *General der Fallschirmtruppen* (General of Paratroops) Eugen Meindl, who had switched to the

A 155-mm howitzer of A Battery, 333rd Field Artillery Battalion, supporting 90th Infantry Division on the Périers sector during Operation Cobra, 28 July. During World War II the US Army fielded racially segregated units, like the 'colored' (in the parlance of the time) one shown here. *(USNA)*

elite *Luftwaffe* (German Air Force) paratroop force in 1940 and then earned his reputation as a fighting commander and the Knight's Cross for his leadership in the Crete campaign in May 1941.

On D-Day most of the German infantry divisions in Normandy were so-called static divisions, formed partly from training and coastal defence units. As the name suggests they lacked vehicles and horses to move artillery and weapons. They were supplemented by *Panzer* (armoured), *Panzergrenadier* (motorised) and *Fallschirmjäger* (paratroop) divisions, whose personnel and matériel were first class but which were often recently formed from training organisations, or refitted and rebuilt after being withdrawn from the Eastern Front. In addition, the competitive nature and mutual suspicions within the German hierarchy meant that there was little co-operation and often poor co-ordination between elements of the *Heer* (Army), *Luftwaffe*, *Kriegsmarine* (Navy) and *Waffen-SS*. In Normandy the German reserves were usually committed piecemeal, which meant that the better-class 'attack' or mobile infantry and paratroop divisions were often interspersed as *Kampfgruppen* or battlegroups to strengthen the static divisions. Given the attritional nature of the fighting, this forming of *ad hoc* battlegroups increased in frequency as fragments of shattered and exhausted units were reorganised to meet the operational need.

The fighting throughout July after the capture of Cherbourg had seen the Germans unable to contain the expanding American bridgehead in the Cotentin. The German units were gradually forced back and had to commit reserves to plug each gap as it threatened to break open. The defences came under pressure at different times along each sector of the front, but initially American inexperience allowed Hausser to react to each threat with what reserves he could muster and then redeploy what he could cobble together to meet the next crisis. However, while it was evident that German tactics could impose delay, they could not stop the Allied advance. In the west Major General (Maj Gen) Troy H. Middleton's VIII US Corps ground away through German defences on to the high ground protecting la Haye-du-Puits, while VII US Corps advanced from Carentan through the *prairies marécageuses* and XIX US Corps fought its way forward onto the high ground protecting St-Lô. In this way, despite dogged defence and great skill, the two corps of Seventh Army were gradually pushed back onto a line north of the Périers–St-Lô road, fighting from hedgerow to hedgerow and using up armour in attempts to regain lost ground.

Winning the battle for supply. American soldiers unloading 155-mm artillery shells in preparation for Operation Cobra, 25 July. (USNA)

THE TACTICAL BALANCE

Despite Hitler's rigid control, German tactical skills were still evident at sub-unit and unit level. The evolution of pre-war American doctrine had been strongly influenced by German doctrinal development and there were strong similarities to the German approach of 1940 in the command, organisation and tactical drills within the American infantry and tank formations.

The 'rule of threes' dictated the American tactical approach. Each infantry division was structured with three infantry regiments consisting of three infantry battalions, each of three rifle companies, each of three rifle platoons, each of three infantry squads. (In addition support components existed at various levels: each infantry regiment included a cannon company and an anti-tank company; each rifle battalion had a headquarters company with, among other components, an anti-tank platoon; and each rifle company had a weapons platoon.) Standard drills provided for one of the three manoeuvre elements to fix the enemy forces and suppress them with firepower, one to outflank the enemy position or attack it and the third to be held as reserve ready to exploit success. Key to this being successful was the ability of the rifle squad to suppress the opposition with its integral firepower; it was here that an essentially sound doctrine foundered, because the basic US infantry squad lacked the firepower to do this against its German opponent.

In Normandy both the American infantry squad and the British infantry section found that they were under-gunned compared to their German equivalent. The reason was that the standard German section support weapon was the MG 42 machine gun, a superb weapon that could be carried by one man and was belt-fed, firing at a maximum rate of 1,200 rounds a minute to an effective range of 800 metres. US troops had the Browning Automatic Rifle (BAR), an accurate magazine-fed weapon that had comparable range but nowhere near the rate of fire. The Bren light machine gun, standard in British infantry sections, was similar. The weight of German fire negated one of the essential legs on which American and British tactical doctrine was based: winning the firefight. In close-country fighting the MG 42 could pin down and suppress its opposition. Weight of numbers on the Allied side was negated by the dense hedgerows; one could only use so many men effectively in a small field. Deploying too many simply increased the number of targets for a German defence that cleverly combined machine-gun arcs of fire with mortar support, making each field an attritional battlefield.

If this was true at squad level it also remained the case at platoon and company. A German company commander could interlock the firepower of 10 MG 42s against an American infantry company with 9 BARs and two Browning .30-calibre machine guns. Even when the number of BARs in each squad was doubled to two, the advantages in weight of fire still remained with the Germans.

On watch with a Browning machine gun, 4th Armored Division, 27 July. *(USNA)*

Infantry firepower was supplemented by superior weight of American artillery fire but at the critical infantry killing ranges, when the artillery fire had to lift, the German infantry's firepower gave them all the advantages. Tanks with their 75-mm high-explosive shells and machine guns could give infantry the punch to suppress the German defenders. Unfortunately, although infantry-tank co-operation in combined-arms teams was a basic tenet of US doctrine, this had not been practised sufficiently.

This also highlighted another technological advantage held by the Germans, the superiority of their Panther and Tiger tanks over the US main battle tank, the M4 Sherman. The Sherman had proved to be very effective against the Panzer III and equal to the Panzer IV when introduced in North Africa in 1942, but by 1944 it was outclassed. The Panzer IV remained in service but about half the tanks in German armoured divisions were now Panthers and in addition there were several heavy tank battalions with Tigers. The standard M4 Sherman's 75-mm gun could not penetrate the frontal armour of the Tiger or Panther at any range while both were able to destroy a Sherman from any direction from up to 2 kilometres (km) away. A total of 102 M4A1 Shermans with 76-mm guns arrived in France in time for Cobra and were distributed evenly between 2nd and 3rd Armored Divisions. These were more powerful but still incapable of penetrating the frontal armour of a Panther. Only by using clever tactics and attacking from a flank could a Sherman take on the heavier panzers.

The crew of an M10 tank destroyer of 3rd Armored Division anticipate the bombing at the start of Cobra. They have reinforced the frontal armour of their M10 with a wall of tightly-beaten sandbags. *(USNA)*

This lack of anti-armoured punch was true for all of the US anti-tank weaponry. The main infantry anti-tank weapon, the 2.36-inch bazooka rocket-launcher, was effective only against the sides and rear of German tanks at point-blank range, and it took a brave man to use it. This was also true of the towed 57-mm anti-tank gun used by the anti-tank company of each US infantry regiment. Once again, while these had been very effective when introduced, tank armour had improved by 1944. The tank-destroyer battalions that supported the US infantry divisions were also undergunned. Both the 3-inch gun of the M10 tank destroyer and the towed M5 3-inch anti-tank gun had difficulty penetrating a Panther and were ineffective against a Tiger. By contrast the German infantry anti-tank rocket launcher, the *Panzerfaust*, could defeat any Allied tank at short range and the increasingly available recoilless rifle, the *Raketenpanzerbuchse* or *Panzerschreck* ('tank terror'), could penetrate 200 mm of armour at 150 metres, more than enough to destroy a Sherman. It was matched by the other anti-tank weapons in the German arsenal, both the 75-mm PaK 40, which was the standard German anti-tank gun, and the various models of the 88-mm gun in Army and *Luftwaffe* service.

The American experience in Normandy built on that gained in North Africa and Italy. The basic doctrine as detailed in the US Army operations manual FM 100-5 was sound, as were the evolving organisations of the infantry and armoured divisions. The evolution through experience of the armoured division organisation into Combat Commands A, B and R (Reserve) gave US armour a command structure that could create combined-arms teams with whatever mix of infantry, armour and anti-tank assets was required.

On the ground Bradley and his commanders learnt the hard way that seizing vital and dominating terrain was an important step to the ultimate aim of destroying the enemy. Manoeuvres which allowed the Germans to retain dominating terrain simply presented them with the chance to use their artillery and mortars to best effect. In North Africa and the Mediterranean, US generals had found it was not always possible to go round or to by-pass defences and that gaining vital ground inevitably involved hard fighting and heavy casualties. The fighting through the *bocage* hammered this home.

Michael Doubler emphasised this point in his important study of the evolution of American tactical doctrine:

'The most important battlefield lesson learned in the North African and Mediterranean theaters was that the combat arms had to work together to win. Despite its heavy, prewar emphasis on the need for the coordination of the combined arms operations, the American army had difficulty conducting combined arms operations.'

Source: Michael Doubler, *Closing with the Enemy*, p. 13.

Talking about it was not enough; infantry, tanks and artillery had to practise the tactical drills and procedures necessary to achieve a working combined-arms team in combat. This had not happened enough in training before D-Day and so this deficiency had to be made good while in contact with a clever and tactically adept defender. Tactical drills involving infantry and tanks working

A 75-mm PaK 40 destroyed from the air on the road to Marigny during Operation Cobra. *(USNA)*

together evolved to meet the threat of the German anti-tank weapons and MG 42s in the hedgerows. Communications between infantry and armour, and ground and air, were improved by having telephones fixed to the rear of the Shermans, so that infantry could talk to tank commanders, and by placing pilots and compatible radio sets in tanks to communicate in a language the pilots overhead understood and use Allied air superiority to best effect. It was a period of intense tactical and technological innovation and the learning curve for American commanders at all levels was steep.

The problem of tanks manoeuvring in the hedgerows was tackled by various means. The standard tank bulldozer blade attachment was invaluable but in short supply. A young NCO in one tank unit, Sergeant Curtis G. Culin, Jnr., experimented with what material was readily available. He welded steel scrap from German beach defences into a hedge cutter with tusk-like prongs. When fitted to the front of a standard Sherman this cutter engaged and drove into the thick earthen bank of the hedgerow and allowed the tank to drive a hole through. Nicknamed the 'Rhino', it impressed Bradley when he saw it demonstrated on 14 July. He ordered its mass production in workshops in Normandy and directed that it was not to be used before the start of Cobra. By that time three out of every five tanks in First Army mounted a 'Rhino' and it gave the tankers a tactical flexibility to deal with close terrain that their German opponents lacked. Indeed one could argue that June and July allowed the US Army in Normandy to hone its offensive skills against a skilled opponent in difficult terrain. When the Germans were forced through circumstance to counter-attack as in Cobra, and then after the break-out in Operation *Lüttich* at Mortain, they found the same difficulties in mounting combined-arms attacks effectively. By August 1944 the American amateurs had learnt from the German professionals and bettered them.

The US Armoured Division

In 1944 US armoured divisions were a mix of two types: 'heavy' and 'light'. This was the outcome of scaling down the tank-strength of armoured divisions to a formation based on the rule of threes, with three battalions each of tanks, armoured infantry and armoured field artillery. This structure impacted on all but 2nd and 3rd Armored Divisions; these stayed 'tank heavy', with about 50 per cent more tanks. and retained the previous organisation of two armoured regiments and one armoured infantry regiment. Armoured divisions of both types were designed to fight in three flexible groupings using the divisional resources, according to what best suited the mission in hand. These groups were called Combat Commands and were designated Combat Command A, Combat Command B and Combat Command R. The first two were provided with their own small headquarters, which was essential once the armoured regiment organisation was removed. Combat Command A and Combat Command B were task-structured and often employed additional resources not integral to the division. Combat Command R served as the divisional reserve with primarily an administrative function but was often used as a third combat headquarters although it was not specifically organised for this role. The two 'heavy' armoured divisions were grouped in VII US Corps for Operation Cobra and could use one of their three regimental headquarters to provide a command organisation for Combat Command R. This was not possible in the 'light' armoured divisions such as 4th and 6th Armored Divisions that were grouped in VIII US Corps for Operation Cobra.

German tactical skills were not matched by any meaningful strategic plan and both in the air and in the logistic battle the Germans were losing. The *Luftwaffe* had ceased to have a real influence on the fighting. It lacked resources and was committed to too many fronts. Some 800 fighters had been redeployed to France in the first fortnight of the invasion but by the start of Cobra over half had been destroyed and reinforcements were running out. Armaments Minister Albert Speer was achieving miracles with aircraft production and in the three months ending 30 June, 4,545 single-engine fighters were produced from German factories. However, they were outnumbered by the 5,527 lost in combat, by accident or from bombing and ground attack. Allied air forces could strike at will over the Normandy battlefields and severely interdict supplies and reinforcements to the German forces.

Reinforcement units, often exhausted by the difficulties in moving forward into the battle zone, were fed into battle piecemeal as they arrived. Up to the eve of Cobra on 23 July, Seventh Army and Panzer Group West had lost 116,863 killed, wounded and missing, but had received only 10,078 reinforcements. It was the same with armour: of the 250 tanks destroyed in the first six weeks, only 17 were replaced. Air interdiction was having a critical effect.

American reinforcements check their equipment before linking up with their units in the build-up to Cobra, 23 July. *(USNA)*

The Allies also won the battle for supply. Despite the loss of the American 'Mulberry' artificial harbour in the storms of 19–21 June, landings across the beaches and through the surviving British Mulberry still reached a daily total of 54,000 tons. One and a half million men were landed in the first seven weeks with their arms, equipment and supplies: a total of 36 divisions as well as supporting troops, logistics and air force units. By contrast 20 German divisions had reached the front in the same period, many without equipment and seriously under-strength, while the Allied deception plan kept 18 divisions of the German Fifteenth Army still in position on the Channel coast waiting for a further landing in the Calais sector. On Bradley's First Army front his supply base could support his four army corps and also the three further corps that were being assembled to form Patton's Third Army.

GIs of 6th Infantry and an abandoned German field gun, Marigny, 30 July. *(USNA)*

The Situation in Seventh Army

On the eve of Cobra, Second (British) Army with 14 divisions faced 14 German divisions, 5 of which had arrived in the previous fortnight, while Bradley's First Army, with 15 divisions and 4 of Patton's yet-to-be-formed Third Army in reserve, faced a makeshift collection of units and formations that amounted to some 10 divisions, only one of which had been in action less than a month.

German Seventh Army had some 25,000–30,000 combat troops with perhaps 117 tanks and some 240 assault guns of all types in line and available in reserve. Kluge was concerned at the structure of the German defence facing First Army, worrying that Hausser had committed his armour to a front-line role when it should be concentrated as a reserve ready to counter-attack when needed. A restructuring to allow infantry to replace armour in the front line was underway in Panzer Group West, but Hausser believed that his infantry were incapable of holding the line without integral armoured support, and so little regrouping was done in his sector.

South of St-Lô, Meindl's II Paratroop Corps consisted of 3rd

GIs of 9th Infantry Division's 3/47th Infantry move forward through a breach in a hedgerow made by a tank-dozer, 25 July. *(USNA)*

Paratroop Division and 352nd Infantry Division, an amalgam of various formations shattered in the fighting for St-Lô, but which, despite this, had proved itself to be a tenacious and gritty fighting force. Choltitz's LXXXIV Corps, opposing VIII and VII US Corps, was particularly thinly stretched. Facing VIII Corps, the flooded coastal sector around Lessay was held by the remnants of two static divisions, 243rd Infantry Division and 91st Airlanding Division, with the Périers–Coutances road sector held by 2nd SS Panzer Division *Das Reich*. 2nd SS Panzer Division was the strongest in Seventh Army with 37 Panzer IVs, 41 Panthers, and 25 *Sturmgeschütz* assault guns operational on 23 July. By contrast the last division, 17th SS Panzergrenadier Division *Götz von Berlichingen*, lacked any armour except for a battalion of assault guns and had been so reduced in strength that it was classed as suitable only for limited defensive missions.

5th Paratroop Division straddled the boundary between VIII and VII Corps in the River Lozon area. Elements of it had been bled off to reinforce other sectors and in effect it consisted of what was left of 15th Paratroop Regiment and reconnaissance elements, totalling some 3,000 effectives. Hausser regarded it as 'of questionable worth' but it would prove its capabilities in the fighting to come. Panzer Lehr Division under GenLt Fritz Bayerlein, a highly skilled tank commander, anchored the defence facing VII Corps. Its had been reduced to 80 tanks, of which only 16 Panthers and 15 Panzer IVs were running on 23 July, and was complemented by battlegroups attached from various formations; a weak battalion-size unit of 5th Paratroop Division made up of an amalgamation of 13th and 14th Paratroop Regiments, Battlegroup *Brosow* from 2nd SS Panzer Division and Battlegroup *Heintz* from 275th Infantry Division. Choltitz withdrew the exhausted 352rd Division into corps reserve behind the depleted 5th Paratroop Division.

The fighting in the Cotentin had in Montgomery's words 'eaten the guts out of the German defence'. General von Choltitz reported that the fighting in the *bocage* up to 15 July had been 'one tremendous bloodbath, such as I have never seen in eleven years of war'. Reinforcements were urgently needed. Hausser, commanding Seventh Army, asked for a panzer mobile reserve and for one or two brigades of *Nebelwerfers*, the very effective multi-barrel rocket-launchers; all were refused as the resources were more urgently needed against the British on the Caen front.

Fighter-bomber pilots of Maj Gen Elwood R. 'Pete' Quesada's IX Tactical Air Command inspect the damage to a Panther tank inflicted during the fighting in the hedgerows in the lead-up to Operation Cobra. Sherman tanks equipped with high-frequency SCR610 radios and staffed with pilots were known as 'Cutbreak' and responsible for air–ground liaison. This link was critical to Cobra's success. (USNA)

CHAPTER 3

FIRST US ARMY

General George C. Marshall, Chief of Staff US Army, had identified and assembled the team that now spearheaded the Allied and American effort in Europe. General Dwight D. Eisenhower had come to Marshall's attention because of his planning skills. As head of the Operations Division of the War Department General Staff in America's early days at war, Eisenhower formulated the strategic concept for the deployment of American forces that Marshall adopted and made his own. His skills in planning and then in working with the British saw him appointed to command US forces in the European theatre. Eisenhower then became Supreme Allied Commander for the invasion of North Africa and then led the invasions of Sicily and Italy, before becoming Supreme Commander, Allied Expeditionary Force, in North West Europe in 1944.

(From left) Maj Gen Elwood A. 'Pete' Quesada, Lt Gen Omar N. Bradley and Maj Gen William B. Kean, First Army Chief of Staff, 16 August. *(USNA)*

Lt Gen Omar N. Bradley, a 1915 classmate of Eisenhower's at West Point, had also been earmarked for high command, as had the more senior Lt Gen George S. Patton, Bradley had served as Patton's deputy at corps level in Tunisia and at army level in Sicily. The infamous incidents on Sicily, in which Patton struck hospitalised men and accused them of cowardice, saw the roles reversed. It was Bradley who went to command First Army in England and eventually 12th Army Group in France. He was seen to have the prudence and judgement that Patton sometimes lacked. Eisenhower described Bradley as: 'the best rounded combat leader I have yet met in our service. While he probably lacks some of the extraordinary and ruthless driving power that Patton can exert at critical moments... he is among our best.'

Patton, however, survived to command an army in Europe because Eisenhower wanted him there. He was Eisenhower's choice,

Lt Gen George S. Patton, Jnr. (*right*), with his chief of staff, Maj Gen Hugh J. Gaffey, 6 July. (*USNA*)

as Bradley was quick to tell him in Normandy, when he believed that Patton forgot who was now boss. Patton had natural flair and tactical brilliance and it was this talent that saw him impatiently waiting in the wings in an apple orchard near the village of Néhou with his Third Army staff while Bradley fought his war and laid the groundwork for an end to the stalemate.

In the same way that Marshall had earmarked those who would command and organise the American war effort, Eisenhower identified those he wanted to command the components of his armies. First in this came Bradley and Patton; however, also notable were his corps commanders, two of whom in particular would be central to Operation Cobra. Maj Gen J. Lawton 'Lightning Joe' Collins, commanding VII Corps, had been identified by Eisenhower before he made his name as a divisional commander fighting the Japanese on Guadalcanal earlier in the war, and confirmed it with the performance of VII Corps in the taking of Cherbourg and the fighting across the Cotentin Peninsula.

Eisenhower saw the same talents in Maj Gen Troy H. Middleton, commanding VIII Corps. Despite Marshall's doubts about his physical fitness, Eisenhower wanted him because he knew how to fight. Middleton had risen to regimental command in the First World War and had shown his talents as a divisional commander in Sicily and Italy. Now both men were given key roles in Cobra.

Collins' VII Corps was to achieve the key part of the break-in and break-through plan while Middleton's VIII Corps would capitalise on Collins' success by driving the German defenders on his front back on to the block that Collins had created.

(From left) Lt Gen Bradley, Maj Gen Leonard T. Gerow, commander of V Corps, Gen Eisenhower and Maj Gen J. Lawton Collins of VII Corps, 21 July. *(USNA)*

THE COBRA PLAN

Bradley summarised the plan in his memoirs:

'First, we must pick a soft point in the enemy's line: next, concentrate our forces against it. Then after smashing through with a blow that would crush his front-line defenses, we would spill our mechanized columns through that gap before the enemy could recover his senses.'

Source: Bradley, *A Soldier's Story*, p. 318.

By 19 July, Bradley's XIX and V Corps had captured the critical communication centre of St-Lô, which until its capture acted like a cork in a bottle to any attempt to by-pass it to the west. Hard gritty fighting saw the American forces close up to the Lessay–Périers–St-Lô highway, with VII Corps getting out of the marshes and on to dry land. These gains offered a jumping-off point for an offensive, with St-Lô becoming the hinge on which it could pivot as well as anchoring the eastern or left flank.

Bradley and his staff had searched for a break-out option since the second week of July, when it first became apparent that there was going to be no easy way out of the Cotentin *bocage*. He envisaged a ground offensive that capitalised on an 'overwhelming bombardment from the air'. Code-named Cobra, the plan aimed to use 'a heavy air bombardment to destroy an enemy defensive position of tactical significance'. It mirrored Montgomery's attempt to use heavy bombers on 7 July to facilitate his attack on Caen in Operation 'Charnwood' and which was tried again on 18 July in Operation 'Goodwood'.

Goodwood had been preceded by a pattern of carpet-bombing to open the way for an assault by three armoured divisions. Although the attack had made only limited gains and incurred serious losses, the bombing had destroyed German armour deployed in static defensive positions, caused delay and confusion among reserves, and had a serious psychological impact on the defending infantry, who saw comrades blown apart under the rain of bombs. Despite its apparently modest achievements, Goodwood had been an ominous portent to the German leaders in Normandy. Kluge conferred with his commanders and notified Hitler of his concerns in a letter dated 22 July. It stressed the overwhelming influence of the Allies' 'complete command of the air' and the impossibility of counterbalancing its 'truly annihilating effect'. Kluge concluded:

> 'In spite of intense efforts the moment has drawn near when this front, already so heavily strained, will break. And once the enemy is in open country, an orderly command will hardly be practicable in view of the insufficient mobility of our troops.'

The apparent failure of Goodwood put a brake on Bradley and his staff, preventing them making over-optimistic expectations of their attempt achieving more than a 'limited advance'. However, while Bradley placed a limit on what Cobra was to achieve, his goal was to establish an opening for his forces to exploit. He wanted to make full use of the greater mobility of his forces and set Coutances as the immediate target which, in terms of Normandy operations to that date, far exceeded in depth anything previously achieved.

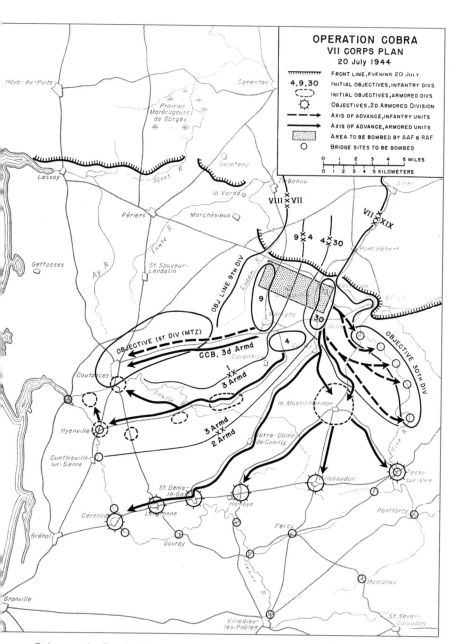

Cobra was Lt Gen Bradley's brainchild and its evolution into the final plan shown here was due to the good working relationship that existed between Bradley and Maj Gen Collins whose VII Corps would put it into effect. The plan was based on an infantry break-in followed by an armoured break-out, with the German defences being smashed by massive bombing. Bradley adjusted the corps boundaries in accordance with Collins' needs and boosted the infantry available, adding 4th Infantry Division from Army reserve. The infantry would break in and create a 'defended corridor' for three armoured columns to pass through towards Coutances and set up blocks against counter-attacks from the south.

Goodwood, while not as successful as Montgomery had planned or wished for, had helped to retain the bulk of the German armour in positions facing the British and Canadians and led to two divisions intended to strengthen the armoured reserves of Seventh Army on the American front, 2nd and 116th Panzer Divisions, being redeployed against Second (British) Army.

Cobra was Bradley's brain-child, but like all such operations its final shape evolved from the interchange of ideas between Bradley and his staff, Montgomery at 21st Army Group, Eisenhower at SHAEF, discussions with his corps commanders – particularly Collins, whose VII Corps had been earmarked for the key break-out role – and with Bradley's former commander and now subordinate, Patton.

Private Peter M.N. Patti gives a wounded German prisoner a smoke, Marigny, 29 July. (USNA)

The First Army offensive was to take place in the area bounded by Lessay and St-Lô, with the northern boundary being the Lessay–Périers–St-Lô road immediately south of the existing front line. The proposed zone of exploitation extended about 60 km south to Avranches on the west coast and inland to Domfront. This area contained no fewer than eight river systems, all of which presented, formidable obstacles to any armoured advance, heightened by the steepness of the valley walls through which they flow. Middleton's VIII Corps' front was divided by the Rivers Ay and Taute, and Collins' VII Corps' boundaries were defined by the Lozon in the west and the Vire in the east. Further south the Soulles, Sienne and Airou cut west to east across the line of advance; the bottleneck of high ground centred on Avranches was protected by the Sée to its north and any exit into Brittany had to negotiate the Sélune to its south. It was a difficult piece of ground that offered great advantages to the defender, but Bradley's intelligence assessment indicated that Hausser's Seventh Army had the bulk of its available resources in the shop window and, assuming that the armoured punch worked, American forces could move faster than German reinforcements could be repositioned.

Bradley's plan involved pressure being applied along the entire First Army front from west to east by each of his four corps: VIII, VII, XIX and V Corps. The point of penetration would be by VII Corps between Marigny and St-Lô on a 7-km front, establishing a defended corridor to allow the passage of VII Corps' armour and mechanised infantry to pivot on Marigny and drive west to the sea between Coutances and Bréhal. This was to be followed by VIII Corps, attacking at H+6 hours and pinning the enemy to its front on to the encirclement conducted by VII Corps. XIX and V Corps were to attack after D-Day and pin down German reserves east of the River Vire and prevent any counter-attacks developing from the east by holding the shoulder along the Vire. Collins' corps would have an estimated 6:1 numerical advantage over the defenders, twice the generally accepted requirement for an attack of 3:1.

Key to the outcome in Bradley's mind was the success of the air strike. The implementation of a similar strike by Lt-Gen Sir Miles Dempsey's Second (British) Army in Operation Goodwood was the direct consequence of Bradley discussing his concept for Cobra with Montgomery in Dempsey's presence. Dempsey had tried it against a German defence in depth on a narrow front with limited success. Now Bradley was to attempt it on a frontage twice the width attempted by Dempsey and with twice the forces.

The air plan for Cobra was decided on at Air Chief Marshal Sir Trafford Leigh-Mallory's Headquarters, Allied Expeditionary Air Force, outside London on 19 July. Bradley and Maj Gen Elwood A. 'Pete' Quesada, commanding IX Tactical Air Command, argued the case for the preliminary air bombardment. Quesada was the apostle of close air support. It was Quesada that came up with the concept of column cover as an integral part of an armoured advance on the ground, putting up ground-attack aircraft overhead in rotation so that there was an immediate air response to any request for support. This revolutionised the method by which pilots co-operated with the ground forces and transformed their ability to provide the air support that the army needed. Communications difficulties were overcome by putting experienced pilots with appropriate radios in tanks as ground controllers so that there was someone who could speak fighter-pilot language and tell the airmen overhead what was needed by the soldiers.

Bradley trusted Quesada because, unlike many of his US Army Air Force (USAAF) contemporaries, he believed in the value of close air support; many of the other air generals believed that close air support, and indeed the ground war itself, were a waste of assets that would be better concentrated on the strategic bomber offensive against Germany.

Bradley sold his plan to the assembled commanders of the Allied air resources. Leigh-Mallory saw it as a chance to test saturation bombing in a tactical role but, while Bradley's request for 1,500 bombers was approved, there was much that was not confirmed and which later would be the subject of bitter recrimination. Both the safety distance and the direction of approach of the bombers to the target were discussed and would become points of contention in the aftermath. The air force recommended evacuating a safety zone 3,000 yards (2,832 metres) deep, an area that included far too many costly-won hedgerows for Bradley to ask his divisional commanders to give it up. Bradley suggested 800 yards (755 metres) and a compromise of 1,250 yards (1,180 metres) was agreed.

Bradley asked for a parallel flight path to the south of the Périers–St-Lô road as a means of guaranteeing accuracy of bomb delivery by giving the bomb-aimers a visible landmark to stay south of. The air staff raised concerns over the intensity of ground anti-aircraft fire on this approach and the simple difficulty of flying enough planes within the time available along such a narrow corridor to get the job done. Both sides agreed that the bombardment should take place and both parties thought each could see the other's difficulties, particularly with the proposed direction of approach. Bradley thought that the parallel flight path had been accepted but air commanders saw this as a service problem for them to decide, providing they achieved an accurate delivery of bombs on target. However, what had certainly been agreed to, in

Collins' words, 'was the mightiest air armada ever planned in support of a ground attack'.

Engineers blasting to clear routes through Marigny, 29 July. *(USNA)*

THE AERIAL BOMBARDMENT PLAN

The VII Corps' attack was to be opened by saturation bombing of the German defences in the break-in sector along the axis of the Périers–St-Lô highway. Fighter-bombers of IX Tactical Air Command were 'initially [to] concentrate on the enemy's forward defenses and then be available for tactical armed reconnaissance and for close bombing support on enemy points of resistance as the advance progressed'. Over 3,000 aircraft were to support the ground attack, including 1,800 heavy bombers, 350 fighter-bombers, 396 medium bombers and 500 fighters flying 'top cover protection' for the B-17s and B-24s.

The plan was summarised in VII Corps' report:

'From H-80 minutes to H-60 minutes seven groups of fighter-bombers were to work on the enemy positions immediately south of the Périers–St-Lô road, followed by 1,800 "Liberators" and "Flying Fortresses" from H-60 to H-hour with a clearly defined bombing area south of the enemy's forward positions just below the Périers–St-Lô road; then the fighter-bombers were to return to the strip right along the road… and from H-30 to H+5 minutes the 390 medium bombers were to hit the same area as the 'Heavies' and then be available on turn-around for additional request.'

Source: VII Corps After Action Report, July 1944, USNA.

On the ground the massed artillery of First Army was to support the VII Corps break-out and this bombardment was thickened up with the guns of those tank-destroyer and anti-aircraft units not required for their primary role.

THE VII CORPS PLAN

Following a directive from Bradley's headquarters, Field Order No. 6, Operation Cobra, was issued by Collins' VII Corps on 19 July. It detailed a 'quick break thru of the enemy's lines between Marigny–St-Lô by infantry and tanks, with armored units exploiting the gap by establishing a corridor and then swinging west to the sea'. The divisions grouped under Collins' command comprised, as

Maj Gen Barton is kissed by a Frenchwoman, 13 August. *(USNA)*

the break-in formations from west to east: Maj Gen Manton S. Eddy's 9th Infantry Division and Maj Gen Raymond O. Barton's 4th Infantry Division, both of which had been involved in the battle for Cherbourg, and the former National Guard 30th Infantry Division under Maj Gen Leland S. Hobbs. Grouped behind them were the break-out divisions: the veteran and tested 1st Infantry Division 'The Big Red One' (Maj Gen Clarence R. Huebner) and 2nd and 3rd Armored Divisions (Maj Gen Edward H. Brooks and Maj Gen Leroy H. Watson respectively), neither of which had yet been committed to any large-scale action in Normandy.

Collins' team of generals reflected the nature of American war experience in the twentieth century to that date. The 56-year-old Manton Eddy was a thinking, fighting, general, whose 9th Infantry Division's nickname 'Old Reliable' reflected the nature of the man. Eddy had commanded a machine-gun battalion in the First World

Air superiority and artillery support were the keys to defeating the German counter-offensive. Here a battery responds to a request for immediate fire. *(USNA)*

War and was known as someone who got the job done. His reputation for caution was anchored on a sound understanding of what his men were capable of achieving. He was a man who went forward to see for himself, leaving his deputy to run his command post. He knew that his most valuable assets were his veteran soldiers who needed to be husbanded. He was quick to defend his men and equally quick in suggesting how things could be done better. It was Eddy who said that the Cobra break-out as originally planned was a lot to ask 'two beat up infantry divisions to handle' and this led to 4th Infantry Division being placed under Collins' command.

Barton's 4th Infantry Division had had its blooding on Utah Beach and had learned the hard way in the weeks of combat that followed. A West Point graduate, the outwardly good-natured Barton was a tough and determined fighter who moulded his division into a first-class fighting outfit. 30th Infantry Division's Hobbs was known to work on a short fuse and drive his subordinates hard, and earned the nickname 'Hollywood' because of it. A 1915 West Point graduate in the same class as Eisenhower, he had shaped 30th Infantry Division in his image as a tough, no-nonsense organisation that would prove its excellence in the break-out fighting and in holding Mortain. His short fuse was balanced by the skills of his assistant divisional commander, Brigadier General (Brig Gen) William K. Harrison, Jnr., a 1917 West Point graduate. Unlike Eddy, Hobbs usually directed from his command post while his deputy played the forward role with the units.

Huebner at 1st Infantry Division started his military career as an enlisted soldier, was commissioned in 1916 and ended the First World War as a highly decorated lieutenant colonel. He had a reputation as a disciplinarian and took no nonsense when posted to take over 'The Big Red One'. He had yet to earn a reputation as a divisional commander, but was in the job because he was seen as being hard and capable enough to sort out a veteran unit that had become too slack under its previous commander.

Maj Gen Eddy with civilians at Beauvain, 16 August. (USNA)

Both armoured division commanders were men with reputations to make. Brooks took over the veteran 2nd Armored Division 'Hell on Wheels' after it had blooded itself in Tunisia and Sicily. Watson was another graduate of the 1915 West Point class and a First World War veteran who had risen through the command structure in 3rd Armored Division, commanding 40th Armored Regiment and later the division's Combat Command A (CC A) before taking over the division itself in August 1942. Cobra would be the armoured commanders' first real test at divisional level.

Maj Gen Barton gives a pre-attack briefing to men of 22nd Infantry Regiment, 4th Infantry Division, 21 July. *(USNA)*

The size and organisation of VII Corps for Operation Cobra evolved during the first weeks of July. Concerns about the freshness of the divisions involved in the Cotentin fighting led to the decision to have three infantry divisions conduct the break-in. Collins balked at having a fourth infantry division attached, though it was decided that 330th Infantry Regiment of 83rd Infantry Division, VIII Corps' left flank division, would be attached to Collins' command. It was to attack west of the River Lozon, the inter-corps boundary, towards the hamlet of Lozon in order to secure Collins' west or right flank during the initial assault.

Collins' plan was to break in by attacking with three infantry divisions across his corps front. On his right or western flank, Eddy's 9th Infantry Division with two regiments in line would attack and secure the town of Marigny and its surrounding high ground; clear a gap between Marigny and the important crossroads of St-Gilles; and secure the western flank for Huebner's 1st Infantry Division to pass through. Barton's 4th Infantry Division would attack alongside 9th Infantry Division on its left or eastern flank and extend the gap between Marigny and St-Gilles, securing a firm base against any German counter-attack from the south, while facilitating the passage of Watson's 3rd Armored Division to break out. Hobbs' 30th Infantry Division was on VII Corps' left or eastern flank. It was to secure an objective south of St-Gilles' crossroad, seize a crossing across the River Vire and hold the left flank against any German attempt to move west, while assisting the passage of 2nd Armored Division.

Once the break-in was achieved, the break-out and exploitation would be mounted by Huebner's 1st Infantry Division with 3rd Armored Division's CC B attached. On Collins' command it would drive through the gap created by 9th Infantry Division and then hook right in a south-westerly arc to encircle and destroy the German forces facing VIII Corps. Watson's 3rd Armored Division was to drive through the gap created by 4th Infantry Division and also hook south-west in an extended arc south of Coutances and drive on to the coast. Brooks' 2nd Armored Division, with 4th Infantry Division's 22nd Regimental Combat Team (Colonel Charles T. Lanham) attached, was to exploit through the gap cleared by 30th Infantry Division: CC A was to secure the left flank down the line of the River Vire while CC B seized the line Cérences–St-Denis-le-Gast to prevent German reinforcements moving north and interfering with the advance of 1st Infantry Division and 3rd Armored Division.

CHAPTER 4

COBRA BEGINS

FALSE START: 24 JULY 1944

Wet weather and overcast skies limited aerial reconnaissance and made life miserable on the ground. Rain on 20/21 July led to the postponement of Cobra, which was set for 23 July, 'weather permitting'. Patrolling was the only activity along the front with limited attacks by the forward divisions to secure positions along the St-Lô road. Patrols reported that the Germans were working on their defences south of the road while making small-scale tank-infantry thrusts against the American outposts to the north, all of which were beaten off. Movement in both corps' areas was 'made even more difficult by the rains which had turned the narrow roads into a thick heavy bog'. Finally, based on predictions of favourable weather for ground operations that would be moderately satisfactory for air activity, Leigh-Mallory set H-Hour as 1300 hours, 24 July.

US and German Orders of Battle, Operation Cobra 25 July 1944

First US Army	**Lt Gen Omar N. Bradley**
VIII US Corps	**Maj Gen Troy H. Middleton**
79th Infantry Division	Maj Gen Ira T. Wyche
8th Infantry Division	Maj Gen Donald A. Stroh
90th Infantry Division	Maj Gen Eugene M. Landrum
83rd Infantry Division	Maj Gen Robert C. Macon
4th Armored Division	Maj Gen John S. Wood
6th Armored Division	Maj Gen Robert W. Grow
VII US Corps	**Maj Gen J. Lawton Collins**
9th Infantry Division	Maj Gen Manton S. Eddy
30th Infantry Division	Maj Gen Leland S. Hobbs
1st Infantry Division	Maj Gen Clarence R. Huebner
4th Infantry Division	Maj Gen Raymond O. Barton
2nd Armored Division	Maj Gen Edward H. Brooks
3rd Armored Division	Maj Gen Leroy H. Watson
XIX US Corps	**Maj Gen Charles H. Corlett**
35th Infantry Division	Maj Gen Paul W. Baade
V US Corps	**Maj Gen Leonard T. Gerow**
2nd Infantry Division	Maj Gen Walter M. Robertson
5th Infantry Division	Maj Gen Stafford L. Irwin
German Seventh Army	**SS-Oberstgruppenführer Paul Hausser**
LXXXIV Corps	**Generalleutnant Dietrich von Choltitz**
243rd Infantry Division	Generalmajor Bernhard Klosterkemper
91st Air Landing Division	Generalleutnant Eugen König
2nd SS Panzer Division	SS-Standartenführer Christian Tychsen
17th SS Panzergrenadier Division	SS-Brigadeführer Otto Baum
5th Paratroop Division	Generalmajor Gustav Wilke
Panzer Lehr Division	Generalleutnant Fritz Bayerlein
353rd Infantry Division	Generalleutnant Erich Müller
275th Infantry Division	Generalleutnant Hans Schmidt
II Paratroop Corps	**Gen der Fallschirmtruppen Eugen Meindl**
352nd Infantry Division	Generalleutnant Dietrich Kraiss
3rd Paratroop Division	Generalmajor Richard Schimpf

The planned D-Day dawned dry but low clouds presented serious visibility problems for the aerial bombardment. At mid-morning Leigh-Mallory, who had flown over from England, decided to postpone the attack for 24 hours, but by this time the bombers

HISTORY

were already on their way. Bradley was at Collins' VII Corps command post and watched them fly overhead at 1100 hours heading south 'and a few minutes later the ground rocked and trembled as they unloaded over the enemy's line'. The Germans responded with heavy flak and the whole of their artillery opened up. The first bomber formation in fact aborted the attack because visibility was so poor; some of the second formation and about 300 aircraft of the third formation dropped their bombs, some of which fell north of the road into American positions.

An M10 tank destroyer moves forward west of St-Lô, 24 July. *(USNA)*

During the previous night Collins' forward divisions had withdrawn 1.2 km north of the Périers–St-Lô road in anticipation of the aerial assault. This was reluctantly done and many units did not fully withdraw the directed distance. The sight of the massed air armada overhead also drew men out of their foxholes to gaze at one of the largest concentrations of planes yet seen in war. Hobbs' 30th Infantry Division received the brunt of the misdirected bombing as bombs exploded among the watchers, killing 25 and wounding 131, with VII Corps suffering 350 casualties in all.

Bradley, Collins and Quesada were upset to find that, while Quesada's fighter-bombers had flown parallel to the Périers–St-Lô road, the bomber formations had flown at right angles to the bomb line along the road, passing over the troops below. They blamed this for the casualties in VII Corps and, in the angry recriminations that followed, Leigh-Mallory told Bradley that, given the complexity of the operation, the same flight path would have to be followed if the attack was to go in on 25 July. An angry Bradley had to accept this because any further delay would allow the Germans to reposition their forces and he was already worried that the bombing had declared his intent and compromised the plan.

The cost of aerial support – a B-17 Flying Fortress burns in a French field after being shot down near Villedieu-les-Poêles, 7 August. *(USNA)*

Collins ordered his break-through divisions, 1st Infantry and 2nd and 3rd Armored, to remain concealed in their concentration areas while the forward divisions re-established their former front line positions along the Périers–St-Lô highway. This involved difficult fighting north of the road because German patrols had detected the withdrawal of the American outpost line the night before and had followed it up. In the fighting, 9th Infantry Division's 39th Infantry had 77 casualties, including regimental commander

Colonel Harry A. 'Paddy' Flint, who was killed, and 4th Infantry Division's 8th Infantry lost 27 killed and 70 wounded. 30th Infantry Division made no forward move as all its effort was focused on regrouping after the losses to its leading units. All of these incidents increased the ground commanders' sense of bitterness at what they regarded as a botched operation by the air staffs. GenLt Bayerlein of Panzer Lehr Division was convinced that he had defeated a major American thrust, and regrouped his defences in depth to the south of the road in what would be the main bombing target area the following day.

Two GIs of 47th Infantry Regiment, 9th Infantry Division, wait in their foxhole prior to H-Hour, 25 July. *(USNA)*

D DAY: 25 JULY 1944

On 25 July, 'just 50 days after the initial Normandy beach landings – a gigantic armada of U.S. bombers and fighters roared overhead and blasted German installations in the greatest concentration of air power in support of ground troops in the history of modern warfare.' The front line was marked with strips of coloured cloth and with coloured smoke to guide the airmen above. Quesada's dive-bombers came in first and 'hit it just right'. After them came the bombers in flights of 12, three flights to a group and in 'groups

Members of 3rd Armored Division's CC B examine the remains of a crewman of a German StuG III assault gun caught in the bombing zone on 25 July. *(USNA)*

stretched out across the sky', advancing on the German positions below with a 'ghastly relentlessness'.

Despite orders to stay in their foxholes, the sight of massed aircraft overhead drew many from their pits, where they stood watching the air armada rain devastation on the German defences. Vehicles and tanks were massed nose to tail along each narrow road leading to the front and so, when the bombs inexorably began to creep north, there was nothing that the watchers could do but run for their foxholes and pray.

The reporter Ernie Pyle was among the watchers:

'And then the bombs came. They began up ahead as the crackle of popcorn and almost instantly swelled into a monstrous fury of noise that seemed surely to destroy all the world ahead of us.'

Source: Ernie Pyle, 'A Surge of Doom-like Sound', *Normandy: 1944*, Britannica online, p. 2.

Dust and smoke soon obscured the line of the road and as this drifted back over the American front lines so too did the bomb pattern. Bradley and Collins could tell that some bombs were dropping short because the blast of the 'shorts' would flutter the curtains of the café in which they sat, opposite Collins' command post where they were joined by Eisenhower at midday. Communications were ruptured and it was only after the bombing ceased that their worst fears were seen to have come true.

Hobbs' 30th Infantry Division, which had borne the brunt of the short bombing the day before, was again hardest hit, losing 61 killed and 374 wounded. Among the dead in this area was Lt Gen Lesley J. McNair, former commander of US Army Ground Forces. Going into battle were the divisions that McNair had raised, trained and tested and he wanted to see how they performed. Unknown to Collins, McNair had gone forward to the headquarters of 2nd Battalion, 120th Infantry Regiment (2/120th Infantry). It was only later that his body was found, hurled 30 metres from where he had sheltered and identifiable only by his three-star collar badge. He was buried in secret, grimly witnessed by the generals who commanded the armies he raised and the men he trained.

View from the St-Gilles spur, axis of 120th Infantry Regiment's attack on 25 July, from the bomb-line, about a kilometre forward of where Lt Gen McNair was killed, looking from the new road towards Hébécrevon, marked by the church spire in the distance. This was the location of a German strong-point, consisting of three Panthers, machine guns and infantry, which stopped 2/120th Infantry's initial advance on the morning of 25 July. *(Author)*

There were other casualties, too. 9th Infantry Division's 47th Infantry Regiment lost 14 killed and 33 wounded, for example. Field telephone wires were cut and VII Corps reported 601 casualties, including 111 dead. There were many combat exhaustion cases, 163 in 30th Infantry Division alone; men who had endured over an hour and a half of bombing around them and who were now in GI parlance 'out of change'. They had given everything they had and could give no more, and were now to be seen sitting or standing like zombies with what a future war would term the 'thousand-yard stare', waiting to be escorted back to the exhaustion treatment centres.

Recriminations began immediately; Bradley blamed the Air Force for getting it wrong again and complained to Eisenhower. However, the reality was that risks were taken on the ground and those casualties were the price of such risks. In terms of impact within the selected area, the bombing had been remarkably successful. Having fought to gain the ground the day before, units were once again reluctant to withdraw the designated 1,250 yards, which one must remember was still only slightly over one-third of the recommended safety distance. 30th Infantry Division's front on the left or eastern flank was where the Periers–St-Lô road dog-legged south. Here both sides faced each other on the high ground north of the road, which offered no visible geographic line to assist the bomb-aimers overhead. Immediately behind the American front lines was a target-rich terrain with its concentration of infantry, armour and artillery ready to move forward, made more so by men clambering out of their foxholes to see the bombardment. Bradley took a risk that in hindsight was an acceptable one, given his understandable reluctance to give up hard-won hedgerows, but this was not yet known as the casualty figures filtered in at midday on 25 July. Hobbs was furious at the impact on his division, but Collins' concern was to get his attack started.

One of the last photos of Lt Gen Lesley J. McNair, taken a few hours before his death, 25 July. *(USNA)*

Fritz Bayerlein recalled the bombardment:

'The planes kept coming over, as if on a conveyor belt, and the bomb carpets unrolled in great rectangles. My flak had hardly opened its mouth, when the batteries received direct hits which knocked out half the guns and silenced the rest. After an hour I had no communication with anybody, even by radio. By noon nothing was visible but dust and smoke. My front-lines looked like the face of the moon and at least 70 per cent of my troops were out of action – dead, wounded, crazed or numbed. All my forward tanks were knocked out, and the roads were practically impassable.'

Source: Quoted in Chester Wilmot, *The Struggle for Europe*, p. 391.

The bombing had seriously disrupted VII Corps' attack but its impact, covering as it did an area 7 km long by 2.4 km deep between the River Lozon and Hébécrevon, held by Bayerlein's Panzer Lehr Division and a regiment of 5th Paratroop Division, was devastating.

Bayerlein had suffered some 350 casualties and lost probably 10 tanks and assault guns on 24 July. He had regrouped his forces south of the road, leaving outpost patrols only in contact with the Americans. On 25 July effectives in the Cobra attack zone of his division numbered perhaps 2,200 combat troops and 45 armoured vehicles. He had positioned several infantry groups in blocks north of the road, with the bulk of his forces in depth down the two ridgeline routes leading to Marigny and St-Gilles respectively. On the left or western flank a battalion-sized group from 5th Paratroop Division, supported by elements of 2nd SS Panzer Division, held a roadblock and strongpoint in depth on the Marigny road. The centre was held by three battalion-sized strongpoints with roadblocks covering the linking roads. In the east the much-reduced Battlegroup *Heintz* of 275th Infantry Division had deployed five strongpoints, each of reinforced infantry platoon size and supported by tanks or tank destroyers and light anti-tank guns. All these were troops used to operating defensively under Allied air superiority, using the *bocage* to best effect. The centre of each defence, whether roadblock or strongpoint, was a tank or tanks 'surrounded by a group of armoured infantry' with the defence built up like a *'perlenschnur'* ('string of pearls'). Now Bayerlein's defence vanished in the intensity of the bombing, communications were lost and critically scarce armoured vehicles were disabled, destroyed or abandoned. However, in spite of the bombing and the artillery bombardment, enough 'pearls' survived to hold up the advance.

A 16-year-old sniper taken prisoner during the initial break-in battle following the bombing on 25 July. (*Imperial War Museum*)

THE INFANTRY FIGHT FORWARD

Collins pushed his divisions to get going but as the attack got underway the initial reports were not promising. It seemed that the fighting mirrored that of the Cotentin Peninsula to date, hedgerow by hedgerow with little progress to show. On the western flank of the bombing zone, Eddy's 9th Infantry Division punched forward with two regiments up. On the left was Colonel George W. Smythe's 47th Infantry Regiment, tasked with capturing Marigny and the high ground beyond. Its leading battalion, 3/47th Infantry, was badly hit by short bombing. Field telephone communications within 9th Infantry Division were destroyed and 957th Field Artillery Battalion lost 13 dead and 22 wounded, including the commanding officer and the operations officer. Smythe directed Lieutenant Colonel (Lt Col) Wendel T. Chaffin's 1/47th Infantry to pass through and attack. This delayed H-Hour until 1230 hours and as the

US infantry of 9th Infantry Division being offered sustenance by a welcoming Frenchman on the road to Montreuil-sur-Lozon, with Marigny beyond. *(USNA)*

infantry made their way from hedgerow to hedgerow they found that Bayerlein's Panzer Lehr Division still had teeth. At 1300 hours 1/47th Infantry's leading companies were held up by a roadblock north of the D29 crossroads on the Périers–St-Lô road.

On the right, Colonel Jesse L. Gibney's 60th Infantry Regiment attacked down the ridgeline through le Mesnil-Eury towards Montreuil-sur-Lozon with two battalions up, 2/60th Infantry to the east and 3/60th Infantry to the west, each supported by Shermans and M10 tank destroyers. Despite 3/60th being held by fire, 2/60th skirted pockets of paratroopers holding out in le Mesnil-Eury and reached Montreuil by 1500 hours. This allowed 1/47th Infantry to the left to by-pass the roadblock and reach the main road by about 1600 hours. By nightfall, 47th Infantry had fought a further kilometre south but was still short of its objective at Marigny. Here Eddy paused while an impatient Collins willed him to push on.

In the centre Barton's 4th Infantry Division was led by Colonel James S. Rodwell's 8th Infantry Regiment with two battalions in the assault, 1/8th Infantry on the right and 3/8th Infantry on the left; 2/8th Infantry secured the line of departure along the regimental front. Despite some short bombing the battalions got away on time, each supported by Shermans of 70th Tank Battalion and M10 tank destroyers of C Company, 634th Tank Destroyer Battalion (C/634th). They struck a series of strongpoints, manned by what was left of 5th Paratroop Division's 13th and 14th Paratroop Regiments, now a battlegroup of barely battalion strength. When the attack started 913th Grenadier Regiment was carrying out a relief and so, while the impact of the bombing was severe, 8th Infantry Regiment found itself fighting through a series of strong platoon outposts north of the road. These proved impossible to by-pass and a tough, confusing battle took place in the woods north of the main St-Lô road. Rodwell was ready to push 2/8th Infantry through, but 3/8th Infantry maintained the advance and by 1800 hours his battalions had reached the outskirts of la Chapelle-en-Juger. It was good progress over difficult country against a determined enemy, but well short of the day's objectives.

On the left, to Hobbs' fury, 30th Infantry Division had its start disrupted by the bombing. Hobbs' division was striking down the inter-corps boundary between LXXXIV Corps and II Paratroop Corps. His was a narrow front because Collins wanted him to be able to punch through towards the critical crossroads at St-Gilles. Astride the main ridge, Colonel Hammond D. Birks' plan of attack for his 120th Infantry Regiment was to advance in 'column of battalions' down the St-Gilles road. Should a battalion be held up, Birks intended to hook round on either flank. However, Birks' lead battalion, Lt Col Eads Hardaway's 2/120th Infantry, bore the brunt of the short bombing, with 12 killed and 70 wounded.

Nevertheless, spurred on by Birks and by the intervention of the assistant divisional commander, Brig Gen William K. Harrison, Hardaway got his battalion moving 30 minutes late at 1130 hours, only to run into a platoon-size strongpoint of Panzer Lehr Division's Battlegroup *Heintz* on what had been the American forward line. Birks ordered Lt Col James W. Cantey's 1/120th Infantry to sidestep to the left and continue the advance. Cantey had to squeeze his battalion through a platoon at a time on a very constricted route past 119th Infantry Regiment. By 0200 hours on 26 July 1/120th had advanced as far as the crossroads immediately north of le Chêne au Loup in a final night move against little opposition by the now exhausted GIs. The road to St-Gilles was open but the village itself was still 2 km away. (*For further details see Stand A6, pp. 115–8.*)

Colonel Edwin M. Sutherland's 119th Infantry Regiment, like the 120th, suffered heavy casualties from misdirected bombing, losing 20 killed and 113 wounded, mostly near regimental headquarters. Despite this Lt Col Courtney P. Brown's 3/119th Infantry crossed the line of departure on the north edge of le Mesnil-Durand only slightly behind time at 1114 hours. 119th Infantry's task was to secure high ground around Hébécrevon, which was the planned axis of advance of 2nd Armored Division's CC A to St-Gilles.

Sutherland's plan of attack was to push his regiment in column of battalions down the le Mesnil-Durand road, across the narrow bridge in the steep valley below la Nouillerie, and into Hébécrevon, with 3/119th Infantry leading. The tankers supporting the battalion believed that, because of the bombing, this would be nothing more than a 'road march'. That changed when the column came under air attack from Quesada's fighter-bombers and then under German artillery fire from the high ground south-east of Hébécrevon.

Fierce resistance held up the leading 3/119th Infantry at la Nouillerie crossing, where three tanks and some infantry dug in on the crest above stopped any movement. In addition there was a lot of artillery and mortar fire. 3/119th Infantry only managed to penetrate into the village at first light on the 26th, by which stage the other two battalions had worked round and occupied it from both flanks. (*For details see Stands A8 and A9, pp. 119–22.*)

View from the crossing over the stream below la Nouillerie, looking towards Hébécrevon on the high ground out of sight beyond the skyline. Tanks and infantry near the top of this slope halted 3/119th's advance for a time. *(Author)*

Sutherland's 119th Infantry Regiment secured the village on the morning of 26 July. Hostile fire still came from the high ground to the south-east, causing 3/119th Infantry more casualties than it suffered capturing the village. Hébécrevon was still well short of the divisional objective of St-Gilles, but the road was now open and the signs were there that the German defence was unravelling.

An M10 tank destroyer with 4th Infantry Division moves forward in support while German prisoners of war move along the hedgerows to the rear in the battle for la Chapelle-en-Juger, 26 July. *(USNA)*

By the evening of 25 July, 9th Infantry Division on the right flank was still some way short of Marigny and 4th Infantry Division had reached the outskirts of la Chapelle-en-Juger. However, 30th Infantry Division's progress on the left flank convinced Collins that it was time to put the second phase of his attack into operation. His instinct told him that this was the turning point, that the defences were at full stretch and, if a further push was made in strength, a break-through could follow. Collins sensed 'that their communications and command structure had been damaged more than our troops realized', and took a gamble, but that was his job.

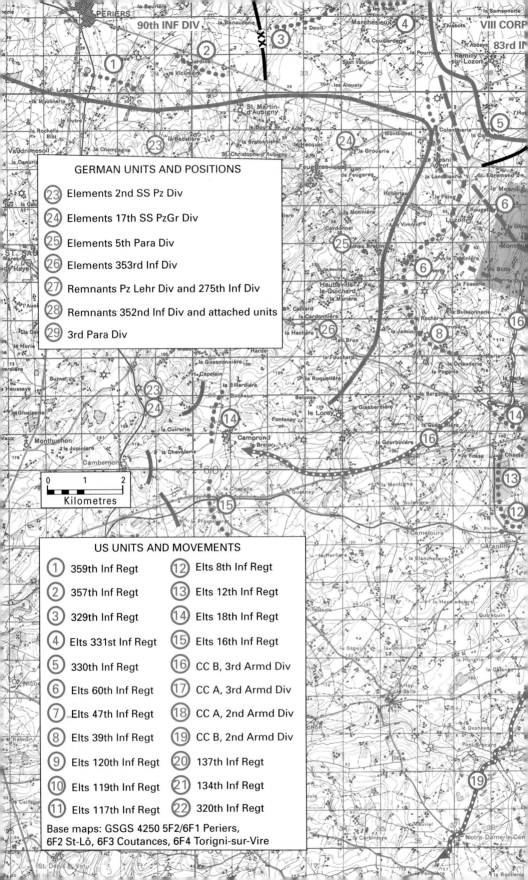

GERMAN UNITS AND POSITIONS

23 Elements 2nd SS Pz Div

24 Elements 17th SS PzGr Div

25 Elements 5th Para Div

26 Elements 353rd Inf Div

27 Remnants Pz Lehr Div and 275th Inf Div

28 Remnants 352nd Inf Div and attached units

29 3rd Para Div

US UNITS AND MOVEMENTS

1 359th Inf Regt
2 357th Inf Regt
3 329th Inf Regt
4 Elts 331st Inf Regt
5 330th Inf Regt
6 Elts 60th Inf Regt
7 Elts 47th Inf Regt
8 Elts 39th Inf Regt
9 Elts 120th Inf Regt
10 Elts 119th Inf Regt
11 Elts 117th Inf Regt

12 Elts 8th Inf Regt
13 Elts 12th Inf Regt
14 Elts 18th Inf Regt
15 Elts 16th Inf Regt
16 CC B, 3rd Armd Div
17 CC A, 3rd Armd Div
18 CC A, 2nd Armd Div
19 CC B, 2nd Armd Div
20 137th Inf Regt
21 134th Inf Regt
22 320th Inf Regt

Base maps: GSGS 4250 5F2/6F1 Periers,
6F2 St-Lô, 6F3 Coutances, 6F4 Torigni-sur-Vire

90th INF DIV

VIII CORP

83rd IN

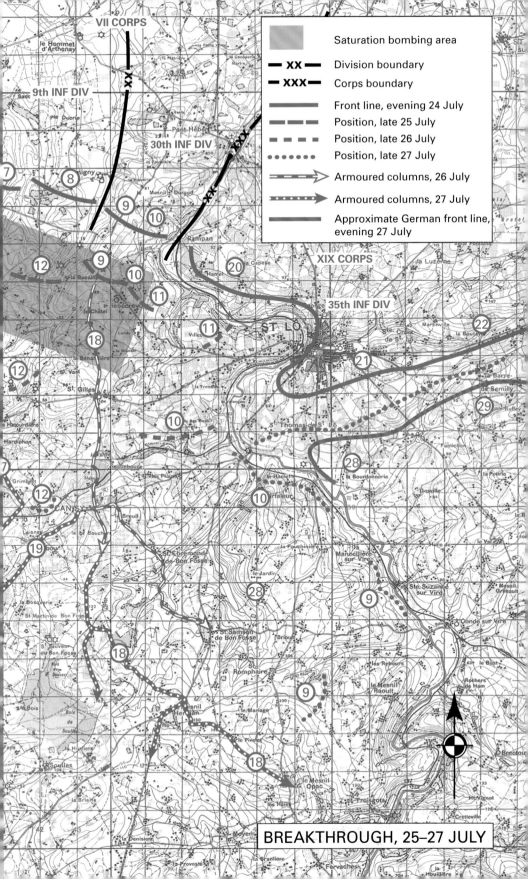

BREAKTHROUGH, 25–27 JULY

Legend:

- Saturation bombing area
- **XX** Division boundary
- **XXX** Corps boundary
- Front line, evening 24 July
- Position, late 25 July
- Position, late 26 July
- Position, late 27 July
- Armoured columns, 26 July
- Armoured columns, 27 July
- Approximate German front line, evening 27 July

VII CORPS

9th INF DIV

30th INF DIV

XIX CORPS

35th INF DIV

ST LO

CHAPTER 5

THE BREAK-OUT

Late on 25 July, both Hausser and Choltitz separately assessed that the American assault had penetrated the main line of defence, but that their line was not broken. Reports showed that 5th Paratroop Division was holding attacks by 83rd Infantry Division's 330th Infantry Regiment west of the River Lozon. The few reserves available were committed to other sectors of the attack, however; Choltitz had sent forward a regiment of 353rd Infantry Division and Hausser a regiment of 275th Infantry Division. Both were tasked with securing the village of la Chapelle-en-Juger and the vital road network it controlled.

Colonel Truman E. Boudinot (partially hidden, next to the driver), commander of CC B, 3rd Armored Division, bringing in a prisoner on his jeep during the fight for Marigny, 26 July. *(USNA)*

Hausser was confident that he was maintaining the line and conveyed this to Kluge. In fact the situation was much worse than he anticipated. Panzer Lehr Division had been all but destroyed in the bombing and the fighting that followed, losing most of its infantry and 24 of its armoured vehicles. Battlegroup *Heintz* and the attached regiment of 5th Paratroop Division had been destroyed in the ground fighting. The reserves committed towards la Chapelle-en-Juger suffered the same fate, being caught by fighter-bombers as they moved forward. The situation was as critical on II Paratroop Corps' west flank. Hébécrevon was about to fall and Battlegroup *Kentner* (from 266th Infantry Division) was virtually destroyed, with Kentner himself being killed. Hausser committed his last reserves, a company of infantry from 353rd Infantry Division and a company of tanks of 2nd SS Panzer Division, to hold Marigny.

Collins recalled this crucial moment in the Cobra break-out:

'Before the enemy could recover I decided in the late afternoon of the twenty-fifth to throw in the 1st Division on the morning of the twenty-sixth, with Colonel Truman E. Boudinot's Combat Command "B" attached, and Ted Brooks' 2nd Armored with Colonel Charles T. Lanham's 22nd Regimental Combat Team attached... The infantry divisions were to continue their attacks to open a gap between Marigny and St-Gilles, but the mission of seizing Marigny was shifted to the 1st Division, and the 9th and 30th Divisions were directed to facilitate passage of the 1st Division and the 2nd Armored Division through their zones. The mission of the 2nd Armored to drive to the southwest remained unchanged.'

Source: J. Lawton Collins, *Lightning Joe*, p. 242.

On the night of 25/26 July, Collins' difficulty was to get his second-phase formations from their concentration areas through a narrow corridor crammed with infantry, supporting armour and the artillery of his attacking infantry divisions. The main push would be on the right flank by Huebner's 1st Infantry Division, which was to seize Marigny and swing westward towards the coast.

Colonel Truman E. Boudinot's CC B, 3rd Armored Division, was to lead in breaking through beyond Marigny and heading for Coutances. Boudinot promised, 'We're going to make a breakout out of the dammed beachhead and it's got to be successful even if it means the annihilation of CC B.' Led in by air attacks on Marigny by P-47 fighter-bombers, Boudinot found the high ground north of the town determinedly held. The town remained in German hands during the night of 26/27 July and it was only the next day that Marigny was cleared street by street by 18th Infantry Regiment.

The German remnants withdrew to le Poteau and occupied a defensive position on the high ground covering the St-Lô–Coutances road while German artillery continued to pound Marigny's ruins.

Boudinot's CC B pushed through down the road to Coutances and by mid-afternoon secured its objective at Camprond. Collins, though, was becoming increasingly frustrated at Huebner's inability to generate momentum on this flank. Accordingly, the VII Corps commander ordered Watson's 3rd Armored Division (less CC B) to drive through the Marigny–St-Gilles gap in a swinging left hook midway between Coutances and Gavray and set up blocking positions on the line Gavray–Bréhal. Brig Gen Doyle O. Hickey's CC A, 3rd Armored Division, led the advance but was held up by demolitions and mines and the resulting traffic congestion was exacerbated by the bombed roads and small pockets of determined resistance. As Collins noted, Watson's 3rd Armored Division, 'was slow to unravel itself'. It was not what Collins wanted and Watson would pay the penalty for this with his removal from command.

Barton's 4th Infantry Division was more successful in the centre against la Chapelle-en-Juger. 8th Infantry Regiment cleared the village early on 26 July and then fought forward across the St-Lô–Coutances road. By nightfall on 26 July it had cut through remnants of 353rd Infantry Division and Panzer Lehr Division's artillery.

'HELL ON WHEELS' – 2ND ARMORED DIVISION BREAKS OUT

The break-through occurred in 30th Infantry Division's sector on the boundary between LXXXIV and II Paratroop Corps, created by Brooks' 2nd Armored Division on 26 July. Brig Gen Maurice B. Rose's CC A, 2nd Armored Division, drove out in a long single column heading for St-Gilles and beyond. Three task forces followed each other south: 2/66th Armor then 3/66th Armor, each with a company of 22nd Infantry; following up was 1/66th Armor with the rest of 22nd Infantry, all of this supported by six battalions of artillery. The breadth of the attack was the width of the road and the fields on either side. The tanks used artillery and fighter-bombers overhead to help push through into the defensive vacuum between the two German corps, overrunning surprised defenders before they could react. Aircraft bombed and strafed St-Gilles, setting the western half of the village in flames and leaving the rest in ruins.

After a fight on the outskirts, CC A rolled through St-Gilles in the mid-afternoon of 26 July and headed south towards Canisy. It was an important moment in the Battle of Normandy.

Order of Battle, 2nd Armored Division
29 July 1944

Commanding General	*Maj Gen Edward H. Brooks*
Artillery Commander	*Colonel Thomas A. Roberts, Jnr.*
Chief of Staff	*Colonel Charles D. Pamer*

Combat Command A *Brig Gen Maurice Rose*
66th Armored Regiment
22nd Regimental Combat Team
 (including 1/, 2/ & 3/22nd Infantry; 44th Field Artillery Battalion;
 platoon, C Company, 4th Engineer Combat Battalion)
14th Armored Field Artillery Battalion
A/ & C/ & detachment E/17th Armored Engineer Battalion
702nd Tank Destroyer Battalion (Self-Propelled) (less B Company)
A Company, 48th Armored Medical Battalion
Detachment, 2nd Ordnance Maintenance Battalion
D Battery, 195th AAA (AW) Battalion (Self-Propelled)

Combat Command B *Brig Gen Isaac D. White*
1st and 2nd Battalions, 67th Armored Regiment
1st and 3rd Battalions, 41st Armored Infantry Regiment
78th Armored Field Artillery Battalion
B/ & detachment E/17th Armored Engineer Battalion
B Company, 702nd Tank Destroyer Battalion (Self-Propelled)
B Company, 48th Armored Medical Battalion
Detachment, 2nd Ordnance Maintenance Battalion
A Battery, 195th AAA (AW) Battalion (Self-Propelled)

Combat Command R *Colonel Sidney R. Hinds*
3rd Battalion, 67th Armored Regiment
2nd Battalion, 41st Armored Infantry Regiment (less one company)

AAA (AW) = Anti-Aircraft Artillery (Automatic Weapons)

The official historian wrote:

'By this act the combat command launched the exploitation phase of Cobra. There was no longer any doubt that the German line had definitely been penetrated. The VII Corps had achieved its breakthrough.'

Source: Martin Blumenson, *Breakout and Pursuit*, p. 255.

Rose's armour pushed on south in two columns, one heading for St-Samson-de-Bonfossé and the other to le Mesnil-Herman, aiming to secure the west bank of the River Vire in accordance with the corps plan. St-Samson-de-Bonfossé was taken during the night. CC A fought its way into le Mesnil-Herman the next day, securing the high ground of Hill 183 (marked as 181 metres on modern maps) to its west on the eastern edge of the Bois de Soulles. On 28

July, Rose's CC A, 2nd Armored Division, passed from VII Corps to XIX Corps on its left flank. Over the following days, together with 30th Infantry Division, it would be engaged in heavy fighting along the line of the River Vire against frantic German attempts to counter-attack the eastern flank of the break-out.

GIs of B/120th Infantry find shelter in a well-stocked cellar in Tessy-sur-Vire, a critical crossroads and river crossing. Believing that it had already been taken by 2nd Armored Division, B/120th Infantry advanced into the town on 1 August. Finding itself with a fight on its hands, Company B fought its way from house to house into the centre of town, only to be pushed out again by mortar and artillery fire. It was not until 35th Infantry Division cleared the high ground on the eastern bank that the position was secured on 2 August. *(USNA)*

Rose's success in securing Canisy triggered Collins' commitment of Brig Gen Isaac D. White's CC B, 2nd Armored Division, as the encircling force. Huebner's 1st Infantry Division was not making the progress Collins expected in the Marigny sector so White's command was directed to drive all the way to the west coast, becoming VII Corps' main thrust. The lack of parallel roads prevented the command's two columns moving side-by-side so the right column, commanded by Colonel Paul A. Disney, initially led the advance, with the left column following. It was a race through Indian country as the combined-arms teams of armour and infantry rumbled down the road with Quesada's P-47s circling overhead.

American officers discuss the situation with the mayor of Canisy, a policeman and the priest, who is wearing a French helmet for protection, 26 July. *(USNA)*

Disney recounted:

'Little opposition was met in the initial stages of the advance. About a battalion of horse-drawn artillery was overrun in the Bois de Soulles and 100 prisoners taken without putting up more than a token fight.'

Source: Colonel Paul A. Disney, 2nd Armored Division, Combat Interviews, USNA.

CC B struck south-west from Canisy, securing in turn Dangy, le Pont Brocard and Notre-Dame-de-Cenilly, which was occupied by Disney's column after dark on 27 July. The advance used a clever combination of forward reconnaissance to bring in air and artillery strikes on likely German positions, followed by armour and infantry riding on tanks or in half tracks. The infantry then went in and cleared the buildings or hedgerows, with tanks giving fire support.

The following day, 82nd Armored Reconnaissance Battalion secured crossings over the River Sienne except for the bridge at Gavray, which was strongly held and became the focus of the German withdrawal south. Disney's right column continued on through St-Martin-de-Cenilly in the direction of Cérences. Lt Col Richard Nelson, commanding 1/67th Armor, was killed during this advance when his tank was hit by German anti-tank fire. Disney's men came under increasing pressure from German formations which were now withdrawing via Cerisy-la-Salle along the road network to the series of crossroads centred on le Pont Brocard, Notre-Dame-de-Cenilly and St-Martin-de-Cenilly. This pressure tied down Disney's right column which had to disperse to secure the crossroads against repeated but unco-ordinated German thrusts.

Brig Gen White directed the left column to secure the road junctions between St-Denis-le-Gast and Lengronne, to block any escape south by German forces . Company-strength combined-arms teams were established covering a network of roadblocks, and for the next two days savage battles were fought against German infantry, and sometimes tank and infantry, columns desperately trying to escape encirclement.

The M7 105-mm howitzer proved highly versatile in keeping pace with armour during Operation Cobra. Here a battery of armoured field artillery engages targets near St-Pois, 3 August. *(USNA)*

On the night of 28/29 July, Colonel Sidney R. Hinds' CC R, 2nd Armored Division, was committed to support White's CC B. During the night the extended ring of blocking positions that CC B had established came under increasing pressure. A block set up by E/67th Armor and I/41st Armored Infantry, 2 km south-west of St-Martin-

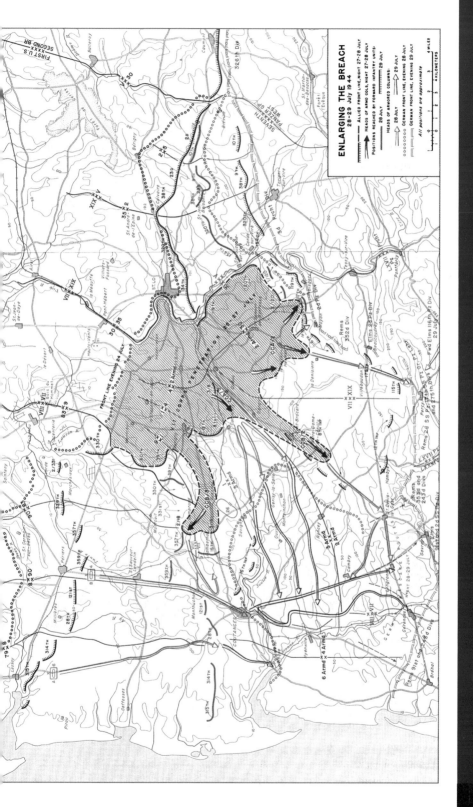

ENLARGING THE BREACH
28-29 July 1944

HISTORY

Half-tracks of an armoured engineer unit move across a pontoon bridge at Pont-Hébert during the Cobra break-out, 31 July. (*USNA*)

de-Cenilly, was attacked by a column of tanks and infantry, led by a self-propelled 88-mm gun. The attack was only stopped when a sergeant shot and killed the 88's driver and gunner with his rifle. The fighting continued until daylight, when the Germans withdrew, leaving 17 dead and over 150 wounded behind.

On the morning of 29 July a German tank column with several hundred infantry overran L/8th Infantry and a supporting platoon of M10 tank destroyers at la Pinetière crossroads and threatened 78th Armored Field Artillery Battalion, deployed around the crossroads. Artillery fire halted the attack and tanks from 1/67th Armor supported by infantry from 41st Armored Infantry Regiment arrived and pushed the Germans back. (*See Stand B4, pp. 129–32.*)

Later on 29 July the left column redeployed and reinforced the blocking positions between St-Denis-le-Gast and Lengronne and also along the Grimesnil road. Hambye to the east was cleared and Lengronne was secured in the mid-afternoon.

2nd Armored Division's swift incision shattered LXXXIV Corps' defensive cohesion. Choltitz and Hausser were unaware that Panzer

Lehr Division had ceased to exist and continued to base their defensive plans on it still being effective. On the western flank, 2nd SS Panzer Division was still able to cover the withdrawal of the infantry divisions, but all communication had broken down between headquarters and divisions. On 28 July Hausser was fired on by an American armoured car near Gavray and 2nd SS Panzer Division's commander, *SS-Standartenführer* (Colonel) Christian Tychsen, was killed by an American patrol.

Wrecked German tanks and transport in the square at Roncey. *(USNA)*

Pressure from VIII Corps and 3rd Armored and 1st Infantry Divisions to the north channelled the remnants of LXXXIV Corps into an increasingly narrow area around the village of Roncey. The town of Gavray and its bridge across the Sienne, strongly held by the Germans, constituted the logical escape route for those heading south but Hausser ordered Choltitz to withdraw his forces to the south-east towards Percy to link with forces that Kluge was assembling east of the Vire to counter-attack and seal off the Cobra penetration. Choltitz objected as this would denude the defences on the western flank but on Hausser's insistence he complied. Once notified, a furious Kluge countermanded Hausser's orders, but it was too late; lacking communications, Choltitz withdrew the remnants of 91st Airlanding Division south but had no control over the elements attempting to break out to the south-east. Large elements of 2nd SS Panzer Division and 17th SS Panzergrenadier Division had already withdrawn south of Gavray, but considerable numbers from both divisions remained in the Roncey area and had to break through the defensive ring. American aerial reconnaissance reported that the roads south and south-east of Roncey were choked with German vehicles. On 29 July, 2nd Armored Division was tasked with preventing the break-out of German forces to the south and south-east. Brooks ordered White and Hinds to consolidate their positions between Lengronne and St-Denis-le-Gast.

Shortly before midnight on 29/30 July, a German attack was mounted on outposts south of St-Denis-le-Gast. Meanwhile, a large German column advanced on the village from the north. The column swept aside an outpost north of the town and engaged and dispersed 3/67th Armor's command post bivouac before pushing on into St-Denis. A running fight occurred down the road into the town, which was defended by B/41st Armored Infantry and some armour. The defenders were driven out of the town in a confused combat during which Lt Col Wilson D. Coleman, commanding 2/41st Armored Infantry, was killed. The German column suffered heavily and its main element turned west, driving through St-Denis in the direction of Lengronne. (*See also Stands B5 and B6, pp. 132–5.*)

At la Chapelle, 2 km west of St-Denis, the German column reached the bivouac area of 78th Armored Field Artillery Battalion, which had featured in the defence of la Pinetière crossroads on the morning of 29 July. A vehicle fleeing from St-Denis had warned the battalion, but the German column drove up and halted along the road that passed through the centre of the position without being challenged. Quick action by Captain Naubert O. Simard, Jnr., saved the day and the German column was wiped out in a frantic battle. (*See also Stand B7, pp. 135–7.*)

Although CC R lost 77 officers and men and some 13 vehicles in this series of engagements, these actions had led to the destruction of the German column and the capture or dispersal of its personnel.

The major action of the night of 29/30 July took place on the Grimesnil road. E/67th Armor and I/41st Armored Infantry, with supporting elements, held the approach to the small hamlet of Grimesnil. This combat team had been involved in the heavy fighting south-west of St-Martin-de-Cenilly the night before. Now, at 0100 hours on the 30th, a strong German column attacked the

One of 2nd Armored Division's M7 self-propelled 105-mm howitzers stopped near a German grave during the breakout through St-Gilles, 29 July. This was the artillery workhorse of the armoured divisions, providing critical fire support to 2nd Armored Division in establishing the break and then containing German counter-attack attempts. *(USNA)*

group on the road west of Grimesnil. The German force included elements of 2nd SS Panzer and 17th SS Panzergrenadier Divisions plus paratroopers and other *Luftwaffe* men, and Army infantry and artillery personnel. It was led by two self-propelled guns.

The first German vehicle was knocked out just metres from the perimeter. Then E/67th Armor tanks fired down the column. After their vehicles were stopped, German infantry continued to infiltrate through the fields and attack from either side. In a fight that went on until morning the defenders finally halted the German advance. Artillery fire was slow in coming as 78th Armored Field Artillery Battalion had its own problems the same night, but it became an important element in stopping the infantry attacks from the flanks.

It was a brilliant defensive battle with superb leadership shown by Captain W.C. Johnson, commanding I/41st Armored Infantry, and Captain James R. McCartney, commanding E/67th Armor.

Prisoners give themselves up during the break-out after Operation Cobra, 1 August. (USNA)

After this six-hour night engagement, 450 German dead and 90 destroyed vehicles were counted; approximately 1,000 surrendered. Given the relative strengths and the combined-arms skills displayed by the defenders, CC B commander Brig Gen White believed that the 'action of this force was outstanding in the annals of our army'.

In the period 26–31 July, 2nd Armored Division had fought elements of more than a dozen German divisions. It is estimated that over 2,250 Germans were killed and 5,000 taken prisoner with the joint efforts of air and ground forces seeing over 539 vehicles destroyed or captured, including 100 tanks, 150 half-tracks and armoured cars and over 100 heavy guns. The division lost fewer than 100 dead and not quite 300 wounded. According to Collins Brooks' 2nd Armored Division 'had done a magnificent job'. Its actions had ensured that a break-out was achieved. It allowed Bradley to transform the limited objectives of Cobra into a major strategic penetration through the German defensive position on the western flank.

CHAPTER 6

THE DRIVE ON AVRANCHES

On 26 July at 0530 hours, Middleton's VIII Corps began its part in Operation Cobra, attacking to the south with 79th, 8th, 90th and 83rd Infantry Divisions and 6th and 4th Armored Divisions. This was part of the pressure that Bradley wanted applied to Choltitz's LXXXIV Corps, to lock it in place while Collins achieved the break-in further to the east. The defenders reacted immediately with heavy mortar, artillery and machine-gun fire along the entire front. Little progress was made on 26 July, but 83rd Infantry Division managed to cut the Périers–St-Lô road before last light.

Engineers of B Company, 133rd Engineer Combat Battalion, use mine detectors to comb the streets of Lessay during the VIII Corps' break-out, 28 July. *(USNA)*

The attack resumed on 27 July and despite delays from mines and obstacles the tempo of the advance increased. It became evident that VII Corps' attack was having an impact on the German defenders facing VIII Corps. 8th Infantry Division cut the Lessay–

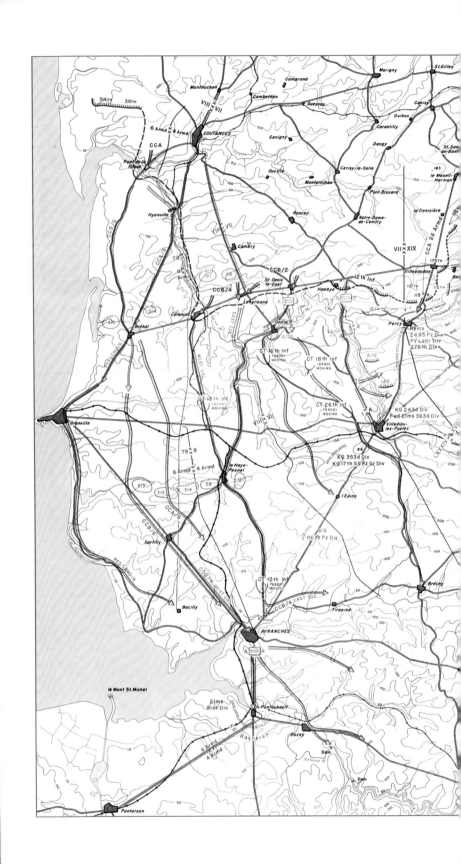

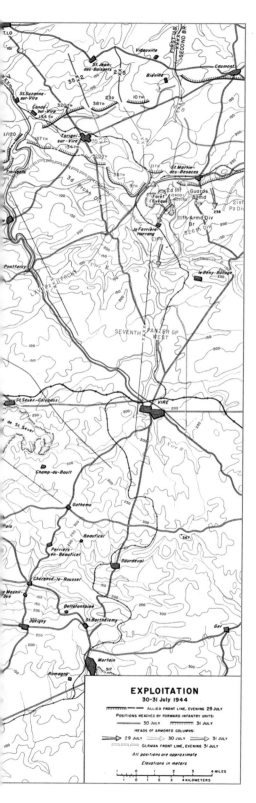

EXPLOITATION
30-31 July 1944

|||||||||| ALLIED FRONT LINE, EVENING 29 JULY
POSITIONS REACHED BY FORWARD INFANTRY UNITS:
———— 30 JULY |||||||||| 31 JULY
HEADS OF ARMORED COLUMNS:
⇒ 29 JULY ⇒ 30 JULY ⇒ 31 JULY
▭▭▭ GERMAN FRONT LINE, EVENING 31 JULY
All positions are approximate
Elevations in meters

Left: Operation Cobra was largely over in three days. Its exploitation reflected Maj Gen J. Lawton Collins' reading of the battle. He sensed on 25 July that the German defence had been hit harder than the ground gained by his attacking divisions indicated. He directed that his armoured divisions attack on 26 July. The difficulties experienced by 3rd Armored Division's CC B in making headway as the spearhead of 1st Infantry Division's attack on the Marigny axis saw Collins shift his emphasis to where CC A, 2nd Armored Division, had torn open a gap south of St-Gilles. This was reinforced by 2nd Armored Division's CC B on 27 July with the thrust towards Lengronne, with the intention of driving towards the coast south of Coutances. It was this that led to the collapse of the German defensive line and the withdrawal of those elements of Choltitz's LXXXIV Corps facing Maj Gen Troy Middleton's VIII Corps. It was now that the total encirclement operation originally planned became a race for Avranches, with VIII Corps having priority while VII Corps kept the door open.

Périers road by late afternoon and by nightfall had reached within 1 km of the south-west of Périers. 79th Infantry Division crossed the Ay through 8th Infantry Division's front and hooked right, capturing Lessay by 2130 hours. 90th Infantry Division took Périers by mid-afternoon and occupied the 'island' of St-Germain-sur-Sèves. It became increasingly evident that LXXXIV Corps was making a general withdrawal along the corps front and 330th Infantry Regiment, still battling for the Lozon crossroads on the left flank, was the only unit in contact by last light on 27 July.

Men of VIII Corps move into Coutances on 30 July. 4th Armored Division's CC B entered Coutances at about 1700 hours on the 28th. There is a memorial to Maj Gen Wood and the division on the D971 where it enters the town. *(USNA)*

On 28 July the floodgates opened. Middleton passed his two armoured divisions through 79th and 8th Infantry Divisions. VIII and VII Corps were now advancing down a narrowing corridor, pinching out 90th and 83rd Infantry Divisions, which would be transferred to XV Corps. VIII Corps advanced in two columns, its momentum increasing as it went. CC B, 4th Armored Division, entered Coutances in the late afternoon of 28 July, where it linked up with elements of VII Corps' 3rd Armored Division just south of the city. The channelling together of both VII and VIII Corps threatened to become a major traffic jam and Lt Gen Bradley directed that 4th Armored Division and VIII Corps would have the right of way, with Avranches and the crossings into Brittany the objectives.

A US armoured unit on the road to Coutances passes through an infantry position at a crossroads, 31 July. (USNA)

It was at this point that Operation Cobra ended. It was now transformed from a limited operation into a full-scale strategic break-out. Cobra had not gained the encirclement and total destruction of LXXXIV Corps as planned, but Collins' execution of Bradley's plan, in particular his commitment of 2nd Armored Division, had triggered the collapse of German command and control on the western flank. Now Bradley was determined to capitalise on Hausser's mistakes.

On the eastern flank Kluge committed 2nd and 116th Panzer Divisions from the British sector to establish a defensive line from the coast at Granville across through Gavray, Percy, Tessy-sur-Vire and Caumont. Committed to heavy fighting against XIX Corps in the area of Troisgots and Tessy-sur-Vire the panzer divisions were unable to seal the gap, but limited eastward expansion of the break-out by holding a north–south defensive line along the Vire itself.

Collins' task was now to drive south and exploit what Cobra had gained. Having removed Watson from command of 3rd Armored Division, he attached that division's CC A, renamed

US M5 Stuart light tanks pass through Coutances, 30 July. First Army's 694 tanks of this model formed a third of its tank strength at the start of Cobra. The M5 was useful for reconnaissance but its 37-mm gun and thin armour made it highly vulnerable on the 1944 battlefield. *(USNA)*

Combat Command 'Hickey', to 1st Infantry Division on the western flank. 3rd Armored Division's CC B, renamed Combat Command 'Boudinot', was attached to 4th Infantry Division in the east and drove south, securing Villedieu-les-Poêles and pre-empting any attempt by Hausser to consolidate a defensive line west of the Vire.

On 29 July VIII Corps, now in two columns each spearheaded by armour, pushed south. In the west, 6th Armored Division followed by 79th Infantry Division moved down the coastal roads through Coutances and Bréhal towards Avranches. Middleton's VIII Corps was earmarked to become part of Patton's Third Army and Bradley gave Patton licence to oversee the corps' progress south.

6th Armored Division's CC A, with 86th Cavalry Reconnaissance Squadron in the van, led the way. Maj Gen Robert W. Grow, the divisional commander, had his first experience of the Patton approach at Pont-de-la-Roque on the River Sienne, when an impatient Patton found him discussing crossing options with Brig Gen James Taylor of CC A. Ignoring Germans on the far bank, Patton strode into the water to check the depth, telling Grow to get his division moving or he would be looking for a new job.

Once across the Sienne, Grow passed Colonel George Read's CC B through on the following day to encircle Granville. In Bréhal, the M5 light tanks of the leading cavalry elements rammed through a roadblock in the town after it had been strafed by the fighter-bombers overhead. The tanks then engaged what were thought to be snipers in the church tower. As it turned out they fired on and killed the French bellringer 'who was up there tolling for victory'. It was a lesson that was not forgotten and it became the pattern in each town for the leading troops to stop the bellringer pealing forth, as the sound was a sign for the Germans to respond with artillery to the obvious indication that Americans had reached the town.

Maj Gen John S. Wood's 4th Armored Division, followed by 8th Infantry Division, punched their way down the Périers–Coutances–Avranches road. Wood ordered Brig Gen Holmes E. Dager, leading CC B, to capture Avranches and secure the river crossings to the east of it. Dager personally commanded his formation's western column, driving through resistance with Quesada's P-47 fighter-bombers overhead. Immediately north of Avranches, Dager's advancing armour barrelled past Seventh Army's tactical headquarters, forcing Hausser and his staff to flee on foot eastwards towards Mortain.

Maj Gen John Wood near Pincy on 27 July. (USNA)

By late afternoon on 30 July, CC B had secured the two highway bridges across the Sée along the axis of the Granville–Avranches road at Pont Gilbert, and at Ponts where the road from Coutances and that from St-Lô joined. CC B then pushed forward up the steep winding road into Avranches. Uncertain of the situation around Avranches and conscious of the need to secure crossings over the Sélune, Wood now grouped both CC A and 8th Infantry Division's motorised regimental combat team under Dager's command.

German columns by-passed on the western flank were now

frantically moving south, often behind the advancing Americans. One such column approached the tank company guarding the Pont Gilbert bridge over the Sée at 2200 hours on 30 July. This column was halted but the American force abandoned the bridge when a second column approached. (*See also Stand C1, pp. 145–7.*)

That night a constant column of German troops, equipment and vehicles passed over the bridge, some heading south through Avranches, some following the course of the Sée towards Mortain. Dager's CC B found itself under attack from Germans flooding into Avranches from the north. Fierce fighting took place throughout the night but Dager ordered Pont Gilbert retaken and gradually re-asserted US control of the town.

Kluge positioned himself at Seventh Army's headquarters in Le Mans but had no contact with Hausser and his staff, who were making their way back after almost being captured, nor with Choltitz commanding LXXXIV Corps. The German left flank in Normandy had collapsed. Kluge's immediate concern was to hold the bridge at Pontaubault. He ordered XXV Corps in Brittany to send all available forces to secure Pontaubault and counter-attack to regain Avranches. This was beyond the realms of possibility as the Brittany cupboard was bare. All that could be assembled from the collection of static and administrative units was the equivalent of a battalion from 77th Infantry Division, bolstered with some paratroopers and assault guns, led by the divisional commander.

On 31 July Wood, at Patton's direction, pushed Colonel Bruce C. Clarke's CC A, 4th Armored Division, south to secure Pontaubault, as well as a second crossing at Ducey and two dams to the south-east of Avranches – if the Germans had destroyed these the consequent flooding would have seriously delayed the advance.

All were secured with little opposition. The German high command initially assumed that the bridge at Pontaubault had been destroyed, but Allied air reconnaissance confirmed that it was intact and undefended. CC A secured the bridge on the late afternoon of 31 July, heading off and dispersing the 77th Infantry Division battlegroup with tank and artillery fire. Despite *Luftwaffe* attacks, the bridge survived to become Third Army's entrance into Brittany.

Patton's Third Army became operational on 1 August 1944, with Bradley becoming commander of 12th Army Group and Hodges, his deputy, becoming commander of First Army. Hodges directed VII Corps to turn east and threaten the left rear of what was becoming a defensive bulge centred on the city of Vire.

An aerial photograph of Vire after its liberation. Known as the 'Martyr Town', Vire was subject to intense bombing on 6 June when bombers in two waves destroyed 75 per cent of the town, leaving 350 dead and hundreds injured. It then suffered in the fighting that followed by being on the junction of First US and Second (British) Armies; the town was finally liberated on 8 August by 29th US Infantry Division. (USNA)

That same afternoon, Wood's 4th Armored Division was rolling over the Pontaubault bridge; by evening it was 65 km away, on the outskirts of Rennes. Patton had already set his stamp on VIII Corps' advance on Avranches. He now pushed Middleton's corps through the bottleneck and into Brittany in a brilliant feat of staff work, with Patton himself stepping in to direct traffic. He made it clear to Middleton that he wanted speed and aggression. He criticised him for not getting his infantry moving fast enough and ordered 8th Infantry Division to back up 4th Armored Division moving on Rennes and 79th Infantry Division to back up 6th Armored Division moving on Brest. Soon he would have XV Corps to deploy, followed by XX and XII Corps; George Patton was enjoying his war.

CHAPTER 7

THE MORTAIN COUNTER-ATTACK

With Cobra's success the battle to enlarge the beachhead was in the past and 12th Army Group was now the dominant player in the ground campaign. Third Army was pouring into Brittany through Avranches while First Army held the door open along the line of the Vire. Bradley was increasingly aware of the opportunities presented by the unhinged German left flank. Rather than push more resources after VIII Corps into Brittany, Bradley told Patton to clear Brittany with 'a minimum of forces' and use most of his army to drive east against the exposed German flank. Eisenhower had come to the same conclusion and backed Bradley's plan.

This matched Patton's ambitions and he directed Lt Gen Wade Haislip's XV Corps to drive on the River Mayenne between Mayenne and Laval. However, Patton made it clear to Haislip that his intent was to push much further on. In Patton's mind there was an opportunity to destroy the German forces in Normandy west of the Seine.

On 5 August, Haislip's leading divisions, 90th and 79th Infantry, reached the River Mayenne. A rapid attack by 90th Infantry Division seized the bridge at Mayenne intact. 79th Infantry Division crossed at Laval, despite its bridges being destroyed. Both were now pushing on east to Le Mans. The German position was rapidly unravelling, and there was no obvious second line of defence.

Collins' VII Corps was now tasked to secure the eastern flank against any German counter-attack. Vital to this was the seizure of the high ground east of the town of Mortain. This was the task of Huebner's 1st Infantry Division and one that Huebner had already anticipated with his occupation of Hill 317, a critical height that was to feature in the fighting over the next fortnight.

The surge forward into Brittany was a chance for the veterans of First Army to regroup after the exertions of Cobra. It was also a time for the Germans to reposition forces to face the threat caused by the huge hole torn in the German defensive line. Hitler was adamantly against any withdrawal, and instead determined to strangle the American break-through by garrotting it at its most vulnerable and narrowest point, which was the corridor between

Mortain and the sea coast at Avranches. He told his generals: 'We must strike like lightning… When we reach the sea the American spearheads will be cut off.' The attack was to be called Operation *Lüttich* (*Lüttich* is the German name for Liège) and it had to succeed or France was lost.

To break through to Avranches Hitler directed the use of the hastily cobbled together forces assembled by Kluge and Hausser and concentrated this into a mass of five weak armoured divisions, under *General der Panzertruppen* (General of Armoured Troops) Hans Freiherr von Funck's XLVII Panzer Corps. Kluge did not share Hitler's belief in a decisive victory but saw this attack as buying time to pull back from Normandy and develop a defensive line.

A dead crewman lies in front of his knocked-out Panther tank near St-Pois during the advance by 3/22nd Infantry (4th Infantry Division), 5 August. *(USNA)*

Bradley worried about his flank and was determined to shore up the line: 'We can't risk a loose hinge.' A counter-attack on this flank had been expected – both Bradley and Collins foresaw such a threat. However, because Patton, at Bradley's direction, had deployed XV Corps as part of an aggressive left wheel heading east towards Le Mans, Collins had to extend his line and shift 1st Infantry Division to the south-east to cover the growing gap. Hobbs' 30th Infantry Division, which had played such an important role

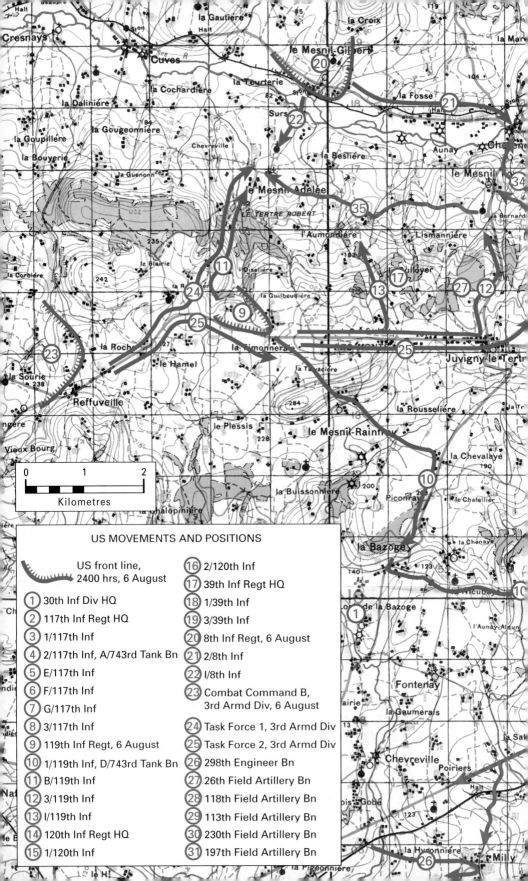

US MOVEMENTS AND POSITIONS

US front line, 2400 hrs, 6 August

1. 30th Inf Div HQ
2. 117th Inf Regt HQ
3. 1/117th Inf
4. 2/117th Inf, A/743rd Tank Bn
5. E/117th Inf
6. F/117th Inf
7. G/117th Inf
8. 3/117th Inf
9. 119th Inf Regt, 6 August
10. 1/119th Inf, D/743rd Tank Bn
11. B/119th Inf
12. 3/119th Inf
13. I/119th Inf
14. 120th Inf Regt HQ
15. 1/120th Inf
16. 2/120th Inf
17. 39th Inf Regt HQ
18. 1/39th Inf
19. 3/39th Inf
20. 8th Inf Regt, 6 August
21. 2/8th Inf
22. I/8th Inf
23. Combat Command B, 3rd Armd Div, 6 August
24. Task Force 1, 3rd Armd Div
25. Task Force 2, 3rd Armd Div
26. 298th Engineer Bn
27. 26th Field Artillery Bn
28. 118th Field Artillery Bn
29. 113th Field Artillery Bn
30. 230th Field Artillery Bn
31. 197th Field Artillery Bn

GERMAN MOVEMENTS AND POSITIONS

- 32 I/60th Panzergrenadiers
- 33 II/60th Panzergrenadiers
- 34 II/156th Panzergrenadiers
- 35 1st SS Panzer Recce Bn, I/24th Panzers, I/304th Panzergrenadiers, 38th Anti-Tank Bn
- 36 II/3rd Panzers, 2nd Panzergrenadier Regt
- 37 I/1st SS Panzers, III/2nd SS Panzergrenadiers
- 38 II/4th SS Panzergrenadiers
- 39 II/37th SS Panzergrenadiers
- 40 III/4th SS Panzergrenadiers
- 41 Battlegroup *Fick* (17th SS PzGr Div)
- 42 I/3rd SS Panzergrenadiers
- 43 II/3rd SS Panzergrenadiers
- 44 2nd SS Panzer Recce Bn

Base map: GSGS 4250 6G2 Mortain

THE MORTAIN COUNTER-ATTACK, 7 AUGUST 1944

in the break-in battle, now came back under Collins' command from XIX Corps and was tasked to take over the defence of the Mortain sector from Huebner. It would have 9th Infantry Division on its left flank, with 4th Infantry and 3rd Armored Divisions in reserve.

On the night of 5/6 August, Hobbs' 30th Infantry Division was directed to move from positions in the Tessy-sur-Vire area to relieve 1st Infantry Division around Mortain. 120th Infantry Regiment relieved 18th Infantry Regiment in and around Mortain itself, with 1/120th Infantry north-west of Mortain on Hill 285 and 2/120th Infantry on the critically important Hill 317 to the east, with the town of Mortain in between. 3/120th Infantry was located in Romagny south-west of the town before being hurriedly ordered to relieve 3rd Armored Division's Task Force X at Barenton, 10 km to the south-east of Mortain.

117th Infantry Regiment relieved 26th Infantry Regiment, covering the divisional boundary with 9th Infantry Division to the north. 1/117th Infantry was positioned in St-Barthélemy and 3/117th Infantry to its west on the ridge overlooking Bellefontaine. It was a hurried take-over; to the front-line commanders German forces seemed to be dwindling away and, although roadblocks were established, no contact was made with 9th Infantry Division's 39th Infantry Regiment north of the River Sée.

119th Infantry Regiment, less 2/119th Infantry, was concentrated in the area of le Mesnil-Rainfray as divisional reserve, while 2/119th Infantry remained attached to XIX Corps' 2nd Armored Division.

Little was known about the Germans. Elements of three divisions, including 2nd Panzer Division, were known to be north of Chérencé-le-Roussel and, while it was assessed that they might counter-attack, the belief was that, in the unlikely event of this happening, the weight would fall on 9th Infantry Division. Discussions with the outgoing 1st Infantry Division spoke of small reconnaissance parties, artillery fire and sounds of tank movement over the previous day.

The German counter-attack was not unexpected but it achieved tactical surprise both in the strength and timing of the attack. Air reconnaissance had picked up indications of German armour north of Mortain on 6 August and around midnight Collins warned both Huebner and Hobbs of a possible counter-attack the following day. In the event the carefully-placed German advance hit the Americans along the junction of two corps and at a time when 30th Infantry Division was not yet established in the new positions it had inherited from 1st Infantry Division. 30th Infantry Division took over a potentially strong position well-sited by Huebner's GIs, but the attack at midnight on 6/7 August found the division not fully linked up with the units on the flanks and without its supporting tank destroyers, which were still moving up. Hobbs later assessed that because of this there were a number of 'rat holes' in the line held by the division, 'the worst of which were around Mortain'.

The German effort in Operation *Lüttich* was made over three successive days. The major attack on the Monday morning,

Order of Battle, 30th Infantry Division
7 August 1944

Commanding General	*Maj Gen Leland S. Hobbs*
Assistant Divisional Commander	*Brig Gen William K. Harrison*
Artillery Commander	*Brig Gen James M. Lewis*
Chief of Staff	*Colonel Jesse L. Gibney*

Organic units

117th Infantry Regiment	*Lt Colonel Walter M. Johnson*
119th Infantry Regiment	*Colonel Edwin M. Sutherland*
120th Infantry Regiment	*Colonel Hammond D. Birks*

30th Cavalry Reconnaissance Troop, 105th Engineer Combat Battalion
118th, 197th, 230th Field Artillery Battalions (105-mm howitzer)
113th Field Artillery Battalion (155-mm howitzer)

Attached units

CC B, 3rd Armored Division	*Colonel Truman E. Boudinot*

33rd Armored Regiment
36th Armored Infantry Regiment
87th & 391st Armored Field Artillery Battalions
83rd Armored Reconnaissance Battalion
B/ & D/ & detachment E/23rd Armored Engineer Battalion
B/ (less 3rd Platoon) & C/703rd Tank Destroyer Btn (Self-Propelled)
A/ & D/486th AAA (AW) Battalion (Self-Propelled)

12th Regimental Combat Team	*Colonel James S. Luckett*

1/12th, 2/12th, 3/12th Infantry
42nd Field Artillery Battalion (105-mm howitzer)
1st Platoon, C/634th Tank Destroyer Battalion (Self-Propelled)

Other attached units
743rd Tank Battalion, 823rd Tank Destroyer Battalion (Self-Propelled)
142nd and 188th Field Artillery Groups
531st AAA (AW) Battalion (Mobile)
4th Platoon, 604th Engineer Combat Battalion

Detached units (all to 2nd Armored Division)
1st Platoon, 30th Cavalry Reconnaissance Troop
2/119th Infantry, 3/120th Infantry

AAA (AW) = Anti-Aircraft Artillery (Automatic Weapons)

GIs of 36th Armored Infantry Regiment ride aboard Sherman tanks of I/33rd Armor at Reffuveille, *en route* to le Mesnil-Adelée, 7 August. *(USNA)*

7 August, was followed by a further major thrust on Tuesday 8 August and what was perceived as a 'dying gasp' on Wednesday 9 August. Five panzer divisions were eventually involved: 1st SS, 2nd SS, 2nd Panzer, part of 10th SS and part of 116th Panzer Divisions, together with a 17th SS Panzergrenadier Division battlegroup attached to 2nd SS Panzer Division. Their total strength was around 220 tanks and 70 assault guns and tank destroyers; 1st SS Panzer Division was the strongest of the five. It was not until the 8th that a fully co-ordinated attack was launched, but despite the absence of the strongest division in the initial strike, it was on the 7th that the American forces faced their most difficult time. 30th Infantry Division was caught off guard; its response was not co-ordinated and fragmented counter-attacks risked defeat in detail. Hobbs later judged that a slightly heavier push would have had 30th Division in serious trouble.

THE BATTLE FOR ST-BARTHÉLEMY

At midnight on 6/7 August the Germans struck. Forgoing artillery preparation, Funck attacked with four panzer divisions between Chérencé-le-Roussel and Mortain. Except on the northern flank, where the attack by 116th Panzer Division failed to materialise, the move badly caught out the American defence. South of this, 2nd Panzer Division made considerable progress and developed a serious threat. It attacked in two columns. The northern column struck along the river flats on the divisional boundary between 9th and 30th Infantry Divisions, taking Bellefontaine then driving on a one-tank frontage along the narrow road through le Mesnil-Tôve until it was stopped by artillery fire and air strikes near le Mesnil-Adelée. This column's initial progress benefited from the morning fog and a lack of co-ordination along the US divisional boundary.

Exploiting its gains was dependent on the ability of the second column to seize the ridgeline running through St-Barthélemy and Juvigny-le-Tertre towards Avranches. The surprise attack here overran the 1/117th Infantry outposts on the approaches to St-Barthélemy. Heavy fighting swamped the defences in the village and forced the survivors to withdraw to the west. Lt Col Robert Frankland fought a delaying battle along the road leading west and managed to re-establish and hold a line immediately short of 117th Infantry Regiment's headquarters at la Rossaye. It was here that the unbalanced nature of the German offensive was demonstrated. A gritty infantry anti-tank defence supported by artillery fire held the panzer attack, which lacked enough infantry support to break through the American line. This came under increasing pressure but held and, as the morning fog cleared, the column of German armour became a target for attack from close air support from midday on. The combination of well co-ordinated anti-tank gun and bazooka fire on the ground and the circling menace of P-47s of Quesada's IX Tactical Air Command and the rocket-firing Typhoons of No. 83 Group, RAF, led many panzer crews to abandon their vehicles, paralysing German ground operations.

Had 117th Infantry Regiment's defence been torn apart, then the road to Avranches would have lain open. It was not. The road between St-Barthélemy and Rossaye became crammed with destroyed and abandoned German armour. This was added to when Funck committed his reserve, 1st SS Panzer Division *Leibstandarte-SS Adolf Hitler*, on the same axis, which simply compounded the problem without giving his subordinates the necessary infantry needed to fight through 117th Infantry's stubborn defence.

Now the air and artillery came into their own. Brig Gen James M. Lewis, 30th Infantry Division's artillery commander, knew that the artillery had not been effective during the initial attacks. However, Frankland's stand with 1/117th Infantry allowed the divisional artillery to concentrate on the roads leading west out of St-Barthélemy. Some 12½ field artillery battalions were massed to interdict the two main roads. This was artillery's most important contribution to repelling the counter-attack. The division had its own four field artillery battalions, two armoured artillery battalions, 12th Regimental Combat Team's 42nd Field Artillery Battalion, one battalion of 155-mm self-propelled guns and one 4.5-inch battalion. These were augmented by two battalions of 155-mm pieces, one battalion of 8-inch pieces and six 105-mm field pieces from 743rd Tank Battalion. What was left of 1/117th Infantry acted like a cork and repelled infantry attacks while the German armour was unable to move because of Allied aircraft overhead. (For *further details of 1/117th Infantry's battle see Tour D, pp. 151–68.*)

Taking cover during the fighting around Mortain, 10 August. *(USNA)*

THE FIGHT FOR HILL 317

Mortain is situated in a river valley, surrounded to the east and west by high ground, of which the most commanding part is the height known both as Hill 314 and as Hill 317 in 1944 (the crest is measured as 313 metres on modern maps). The town is nestled on its lower slopes, which climb steeply out of the valley floor to the east and north-east. The heights were the key to any defensive arrangement and should the Germans counter-attack then Hill 317 would have to be held at all costs.

It was in and around Mortain that the German attack made the most progress. 2nd SS Panzer Division overran the town and set up blocking positions on the road to St-Hilaire-du-Harcouët. This thrust was the main concern for the initially complacent VII Corps headquarters. However, it failed to capture Hill 317, where 2/120th Infantry, less its commanding officer who had been trapped and was later captured in the town, held out under the command of Captain Reynold C. Erickson. His defence, and the presence of two artillery observation officers, meant that the Germans held the valley but remained under constant fire from American positions holding the key terrain above them. Despite repeated attempts by the 17th SS Division battlegroup, the GIs held the hill. They depended on supply by parachute, although much of this fell outside the perimeter, and the delivery of critical medical supplies in hollowed-out artillery shells designed for distributing propaganda leaflets.

An advanced medical station at Mortain during Operation *Lüttich. (USNA)*

On 7 August Collins adjusted his defence. He received 2nd Armored Division, less CC A, and 35th Infantry Division, which he used to secure Barenton, thus putting pressure on Funck's southern flank. Similarly, Eddy's 9th Infantry Division put pressure on the northern flank while 4th and 30th Infantry Divisions, each reinforced by a combat command from 2nd Armored Division, held the centre. It took some time for this combat power to develop but during this time the Germans were frustrated by 2/120th Infantry's defence of Hill 317 and, equally importantly, the holding of the critical roadblock at the road bridge over the railway lines at Abbaye Blanche to the north of Mortain. This, and 117th Infantry

Regiment's defence at St-Barthélemy, held the German thrust. On the ground it was primarily a 30th Infantry Division battle, which was made possible by the effectiveness of the close air support, the critical factor in blunting and then destroying the German attack.

Hitler was furious at the failure of *Lüttich* to make headway. He released further resources and directed Kluge to mount a renewed counter-attack, led by Hitler's original choice to command *Lüttich*, *General der Panzertruppen* Heinrich Eberbach, commanding Fifth Panzer Army. Two panzer corps were to take part, with a start date planned for 11 August. Eberbach formed Panzer Group *Eberbach* to carry out the operation, but none of this was realistic. On the morning of 8 August First Canadian Army launched Operation 'Totalize', aimed at Falaise, just when scarce panzer resources were being withdrawn from the British front. Equally concerning was Patton's capture of Le Mans and the growing threat to Alençon with its critical supply dumps.

GIs of 120th Infantry Regiment in the streets of Mortain, 12 August. *(USNA)*

On 11 August, 35th Infantry Division drove 2nd SS Panzer Division from its positions south-west of Mortain and on the following day linked up with the defenders on Hill 317. 2/120th

A combined-arms team of infantry and armour engages German positions near Barenton during Operation *Lüttich*, 9 August. The nearest vehicle is an M8 HMC armed with a short-barrel 75-mm howitzer while the tank in the middle distance is a Sherman armed with a 76-mm gun. *(USNA)*

Infantry was awarded a Presidential Unit Citation and each of its company commanders received the Distinguished Service Cross. On the same day Kluge received Hitler's permission for 'a minor withdrawal of the front between Sourdeval and Mortain' in order to meet the threat of XV Corps on Alençon.

POSTSCRIPT ON MORTAIN

The American defence of Mortain, although initially lacking in co-ordination in both Hobbs' 30th Infantry Division headquarters and in Collins VII Corps, demonstrated the growing skills of the American GI in combat. The defence of Hill 317 and the fight for St-Barthélemy are small-unit actions worthy of close study for the leadership demonstrated within battalions, companies and platoons; they also offer textbook examples of co-ordinated anti-tank defence and ground–air co-operation. Despite initial faltering at division and corps, the battle for Mortain showed how effective the combined-arms team had become and the willingness of GIs to stand and fight in circumstances that would have seen them fall back a month earlier.

During Operation Cobra and in response to the German counter-attack of Operation *Lüttich* we see the growing evolution in the US Army of what Michael Doubler has termed the 'series of key tactical and technical adaptions... that transformed ground units into powerful, cohesive combined arms formations capable of generating awesome firepower and effective ground maneuver.'

A soldier stands opposite Mortain's Place des Arcades on 13 August, looking at the information board extolling the virtues of the now-ruined town. The effects of the battle can be seen all around. *(USNA)*

Central to this development was Lt Gen Bradley and his First Army. Bradley and his staff conceived the Cobra plan. Collins' VII Corps put it into effect and, although it evolved differently to what was intended, as battles always do, its success showed Collins' tactical brilliance. In the same way, Bradley at his level also continued to read the battle and generated a depth of penetration with Middleton's VIII Corps that turned Cobra from a tactical success into a strategic victory. Patton's exploits have overshadowed those of both Bradley and Collins, but it was their achievement in Cobra that presented him with the stage on which he triumphed.

PART THREE

BATTLEFIELD
TOURS

GENERAL TOURING INFORMATION

Normandy is a thriving holiday area, with some beautiful countryside, excellent beaches and very attractive architecture (particularly in the case of religious buildings). It was also, of course, the scene of heavy fighting in 1944, and this has had a considerable impact on the tourist industry. To make the most of your trip, especially if you intend visiting non-battlefield sites, we strongly recommend you purchase one of the general Normandy guidebooks that are commonly available. These include: *Michelin Green Guide: Normandy*; *Thomas Cook Travellers: Normandy*; *The Rough Guide to Brittany and Normandy*; *Lonely Planet: Normandy*.

TRAVEL REQUIREMENTS

First, make sure you have the proper documentation to enter France as a tourist. Citizens of European Union countries, including Great Britain, should not usually require visas, but will need to carry and show their passports. Others should check with the French Embassy in their own country before travelling. British citizens should also fill in and take Form E111 (available from main post offices), which deals with entitlement to medical treatment, and all should consider taking out comprehensive travel insurance. France is part of the Eurozone, and you should also check exchange rates before travelling.

GETTING THERE

The most direct routes from the UK to Lower Normandy are by ferry from Portsmouth to Ouistreham (near Caen), and from Portsmouth or Poole to Cherbourg. Depending on which you choose, and whether you travel by day or night, the crossing takes between four and seven hours. Alternatively, you can sail to Le Havre, Boulogne or Calais and drive the rest of the way. (Travel time from Calais to Caen is about four hours; motorway and bridge

Above: Notre-Dame cathedral in the centre of Coutances. The cathedral escaped serious damage in the fighting though Allied bombing on 6 June devastated the town, causing many civilian casualties and emptying the city as its citizens sought refuge in the surrounding countryside. *(Author)*

Page 97: Infantry fighting around Mortain consisted of the battle for hedgerows, but it was here that the GIs beat the attacking Germans at their own game in a grim struggle to control the high ground. *(USNA)*

tolls may be payable depending on the exact route taken.) Another option is to use the Channel Tunnel. Whichever way you decide to travel, early booking is advised, especially during the summer months.

Although you can of course hire motor vehicles in Normandy, the majority of visitors from the UK or other EU countries will probably take their own. If you do so, you will also need to take: a full driving licence; your vehicle registration document; a certificate of motor insurance valid in France (your insurer will advise on this); spare headlight and indicator bulbs; headlight beam adjusters or tape; a warning triangle; and a sticker or number plate identifying which country the vehicle is registered in. Visitors from

The monument to Operation Cobra, visited at Stand A2. General Bradley's initials are unfortunately wrongly given as D.N. *(Author)*

elsewhere should consult a motoring organisation in their home country for details of the documents and other items they will require.

Normandy's road system is well developed, although there are still a few choke points, especially around the larger towns during rush hour and in the holiday season. As a general guide, in clear conditions it is possible to drive from Cherbourg to Caen in less than two hours and in less than an hour and a half from Cherbourg to Coutances or St-Lô

ACCOMMODATION

Accommodation in Normandy is plentiful and diverse, from cheap campsites to five-star hotels in glorious châteaux. Caen, for example, has over 60 hotels (as well as such other facilities as restaurants and museums). However, early booking is advised if you wish to travel between June and August. Useful contacts include:

French Travel Centre, 178 Piccadilly, London W1V 0AL;
tel: 0870 830 2000; web: www.raileurope.co.uk
French Tourist Authority, 444 Madison Avenue, New York,
NY 10022 (other offices in Chicago, Los Angeles and Miami);
web: www.francetourism.com
Calvados Tourisme, Place du Canada, 14000 Caen;
tel: +33 (0)2 31 86 53 30; web: www.calvados-tourisme.com
Maison du Tourisme de Cherbourg et du Haut-Cotentin,
2 Quai Alexandre III, 50100 Cherbourg-Octeville;
tel: +33 (0)2 33 93 52 02; web: www.ot-cherbourg-cotentin.fr
Office de Tourisme d'Avranches, 2 Rue du Général de Gaulle,
50300 Avranches; tel: +33 (0)2 33 58 00 22;
web: www.ville-avranches.fr
Office de Tourisme de Coutances, Place Georges Leclerc,
50200 Coutances; tel: +33 (0)2 33 19 08 10;
web: www.ville-coutances.fr

Office de Tourisme de Mortain, Rue Bourglopin, 50140
  Mortain; tel: +33 (0)2 33 59 19 74; web: www.ville-mortain.fr
Gîtes de France, La Maison des Gîtes de France et du Tourisme
  Vert, 59 Rue Saint-Lazare, 75 439 Paris Cedex 09;
  tel: +33 (0)1 49 70 75 75; web: www.gites-de-france.fr

BATTLEFIELD TOURING

Each volume in the 'Battle Zone Normandy' series contains three
or more battlefield tours. These are intended to last from a few
hours to a full day apiece. Some are best undertaken using motor
transport, others should be done on foot, and many involve a mixture of the two. Owing to its excellent infrastructure and relatively gentle topography, Normandy also makes a good location for a cycling holiday; indeed, some of our tours are ideally suited to this method.

One of the series of *Cobra – la Percée* signposts, this example being at the Marigny German cemetery. The significance of each site is detailed in French and English on the reverse. *(Author)*

In every case the tour author has visited the area concerned recently, so the information presented should be accurate and reasonably up to date. Nevertheless land use, infrastructure and rights of way can change, sometimes at short notice. If you encounter difficulties in following any tour, we would very much like to hear about it, so we can incorporate changes in future editions. Your comments should be sent to the publisher at the address provided at the front of this book.

  To derive maximum value and enjoyment from the tours, we
suggest you equip yourself with the following items:

- Appropriate maps. European road atlases can be purchased from a wide range of locations outside France. However, for navigation within Normandy, the French Institut Géographique National (IGN) produces maps at a variety of scales (www.ign.fr). The 1:100,000 series ('Top 100') is particularly useful when driving over larger distances as you will need to do in this series of tours; sheet 06 (Caen–Cherbourg), 16 (Rennes–Granville) and 17 (Laval–Argentan) are needed and will get you from the invasion beaches to Mortain. For pinpointing locations precisely, the current IGN 1:25,000 Série Bleue is best (we use extracts from this series for the tour maps in this book). The sheets required for the area discussed in the tours in this volume are 1212ET La Haye-du-Puits.Lessay, 1312O Périers, 1312E Carentan, 1313E St-Lô, 1313O St-Sauveur-Lendelin, 1314E Villedieu-les-Poêles, 1215ET Avranches.Granville, 1314O Gavray, 1414O St-Sever-Calvados, 1414E Vire, 1315E Ducey, 1415O Sourdeval.Mortain, 1415E Tinchebray. These can be bought in many places in Normandy. They can also be ordered in the UK from some bookshops, or from specialist dealers such as the Hereford Map Centre, 24–25 Church Street, Hereford HR1 2LR; tel: 01432 266322; web: <www.themapcentre.com>. Allow at least a fortnight's notice, although some maps may be in stock.
- Lightweight waterproof clothing and robust footwear are essential, especially for touring in the countryside.
- Take a compass, provided you know how to use one!
- A camera and spare films/memory cards.
- A notebook to record what you have photographed.
- A French dictionary and/or phrasebook. (English is widely spoken in the coastal area, but is much less common inland.)
- Food and drink. Although you are never very far in Normandy from a shop, restaurant or *tabac*, many of the tours do not pass directly by such facilities. It is therefore sensible to take some light refreshment with you.
- Binoculars. Most officers and some other ranks carried binoculars in 1944. Taking a pair adds a surprising amount of verisimilitude to the touring experience.

SOME DO'S AND DON'TS

Battlefield touring can be an extremely interesting and even emotional experience, especially if you have read something about the battles beforehand. In addition, it is fair to say that residents of Normandy are used to visitors, among them battlefield tourers, and generally will do their best to help if you encounter problems. However, many of the tours in the 'Battle Zone Normandy' series are off the beaten track, and you can expect some puzzled looks from the locals, especially inland. In all cases we have tried to ensure that tours are on public land, or viewable from public rights of way. However, in the unlikely event that you are asked to leave a site, do so immediately and by the most direct route.

A German prisoner taken by 1/8th Infantry with a surrender leaflet, 25 July. Leaflets like this were one of many measures employed by Allied psychological warfare units to break German morale during the Normandy campaign. *(USNA)*

In addition: **Never remove 'souvenirs' from the battlefields.** Even today it is not unknown for farmers to turn up relics of the 1944 fighting. Taking these without permission may not only be illegal, but can be extremely dangerous. It also ruins the site for genuine battlefield archaeologists. Anyone returning from France should also remember customs regulations on the import of weapons and ammunition of any kind.

Be especially careful when investigating fortifications. Some of the more frequently-visited sites are well preserved, and several of them have excellent museums. However, both along the coast and inland there are numerous positions that have been left to decay, and which carry risks for the unwary. In particular, remember that many of these places were the scenes of heavy fighting or subsequent demolitions, which may have caused severe (and sometimes invisible) structural damage. Coastal erosion has also undermined the foundations of a number of shoreline defences. Under no circumstances should underground bunkers, chambers and tunnels be entered, and care should always be taken when examining above-ground structures. If in any doubt, stay away.

Beware of hunting (shooting) areas (signposted *Chasse Gardée*). Do not enter these, even if they offer a short cut to your destination. Similarly, Normandy contains a number of restricted areas (military facilities and wildlife reserves), which should be avoided. Watch out, too, for temporary footpath closures, especially along sections of coastal cliffs.

If using a motor vehicle, keep your eyes on the road. There are many places to park, even on minor routes, and it is always better to turn round and retrace your path than to cause an accident. In rural areas avoid blocking entrances and driving along farm tracks; again, it is better to walk a few hundred metres than to cause damage and offence.

A priest of Notre-Dame cathedral in Coutances explains to a French liaison officer attached to 4th Armored Division that all the citizens have evacuated the city because of the bombing. *(USNA)*

In addition to the above, various points specific to this volume should be raised.

The five tours are focussed on the events of late July and early August 1944 and concentrate on the break-in battle along the D900 road between le Mesnil-Eury and Hébécrevon; the initial break-out through Canisy in the direction of Lengronne; and then the drive on Avranches and on into Brittany, followed by the German attempt to contain the collapse with the counter-offensive at Mortain.

Within each tour there are parallel stories that cannot be told within the scope of the book. The tough fighting along the Vire by

Brig Gen Maurice Rose's Combat Command A, 2nd Armored Division, and by Hobbs' 30th Infantry Division is not explored in these tours, but if one has the time, the route to Vire through Troisgots, and Tessy-sur-Vire offers the chance to visit battlefields, historic towns and abbeys.

OTHER ATTRACTIONS

There is much to see and enjoy in parallel with each tour. One should not drive through Lessay without visiting the abbey or Coutances without entering the Notre-Dame cathedral and pausing for coffee in the square. Exploring Mont St-Michel is a natural postscript to completing Tour C. The Abbaye Blanche, used as a medical post by the Germans during the fighting around Mortain, is a must while doing Tour E. Time must be allowed to window-shop in Coutances, to ferret through the back streets in Villedieu-les-Poêles or to admire the gardens of the Hôtel de la Croix d'Or

A memorial in Périers to those of the town who fought in the Resistance. (Author)

in Avranches. Throwing in the delights of open sandy beaches stretching away into the distance or country walks, it would be selfish to devote one's time in Normandy to battlefields alone.

Accommodation ranges from campsites and pensions to hotels suited to every pocket. I found that I could meet my wife's preference for the beaches while I reconnoitred the tours with a wide choice of inexpensive *auberges* and hotels that offered clean rooms with excellent facilities and welcoming hosts.

These tours explores some of the Manche *département*'s by-ways. While taking sustenance with you is always recommended, you will usually find somewhere pleasant to buy food and drink: a bistro in St-Gilles, a bar and restaurant in Grismesnil, a small hotel in a pleasant square in le Neufbourg. These and the many small villages *en route* usually offer the delights of relaxing in congenial surroundings. This is but one of the Normandy's many pleasures.

BATTLEFIELD TOURS

TOUR A

THE BOMBARDMENT AND BREAK-IN

OBJECTIVE: This tour covers the start of Operation Cobra on 24–26 July 1944, particularly the 2.4 km by 7 km rectangle of ground between the River Lozon and the village of Hébécrevon, which was the bomb zone for the break-in bombardment.

DURATION/SUITABILITY: This tour takes a day and covers a total distance of 45 km. The tour is suitable for cyclists, and for those with mobility difficulties as all points are accessible by car.

Stand A1: The Road to Marigny

DIRECTIONS: Start at the car park next to the 'Tough Ombres' Memorial to the 90th US Infantry Division (*illustrated on p. 1*) between the church and the *hôtel de ville* (town hall) in the Périers town square. Drive east on the D900 in the direction of St-Lô through the flat former marshlands east of Périers. Pass over the unmarked River Lozon, then climb up to the small hamlet of le Mesnil-Eury on the skyline. At the junction with the D29 to Marigny, marked by a *Cobra – la Percée* (*la percée* = the break-through) signpost, stop and park on the D900, facing towards St-Lô (east). It is a very busy road so be careful of traffic. Walk back to the junction.

THE ACTION: The D900 marked the northern bomb line for the bombardment that hit the Germans defending this crossroads on 24–25 July. What is now the D29, running south to Marigny via Montreuil-sur-Lozon, was 9th Infantry Division's axis. 9th Infantry Division was to secure the right flank of Collins' break-out by taking high ground south of Marigny, thus opening the way for 1st Infantry Division, with 3rd Armored Division's CC B under command, to push through and head for Coutances.

9th Infantry Division's boundaries were the River Lozon to the west and the D89 to the east. As one can see, any progress south along the D29 depended on securing the ridge 800 metres to the

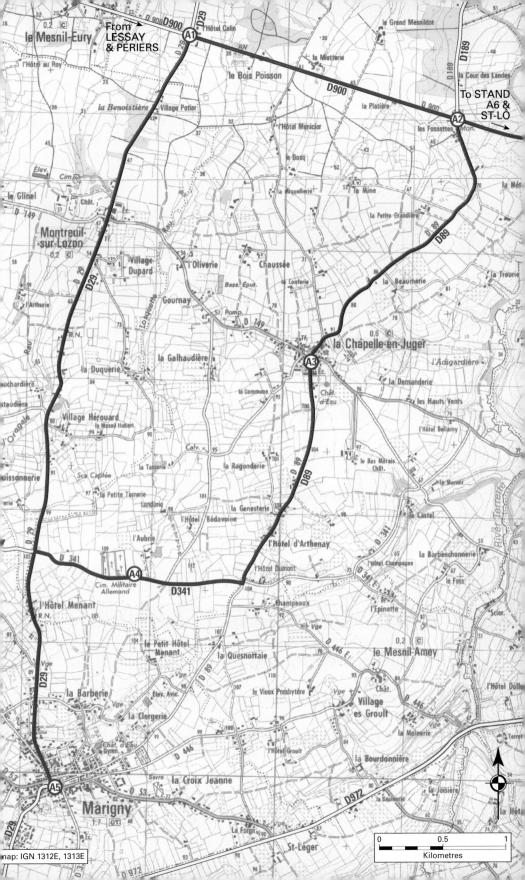

west on which le Mesnil-Eury stands. This was the objective of 60th Infantry Regiment, which attacked down the ridgeline from the north against the village, held by elements of 5th Paratroop Division including 15th Paratroop Regiment. Beyond that again is the River Lozon; west of the river, 330th Infantry Regiment attacked to capture the D94/D900 crossroads and secure VII Corps' flank.

The River Lozon, really an insignificant stream in a broad river marsh, awkward for tanks, marked the corps boundary. The hamlet of le Mesnil-Eury is on the skyline ahead. This was the area where 60th Infantry Regiment made the greatest gains on 25 July. *(Author)*

You are standing on the axis of attack of Colonel George W. Smythe's 47th Infantry Regiment, which was to capture Marigny and then seize the high ground astride the D972 between St-Lô and Coutances. On the morning of 25 July, however, the leading battalion, 3/47th Infantry, was badly hit by short bombing. The bomb line along the D900 where you are standing was obscured by smoke and the bombs started to fall across the highway and north along the D29. Despite directions to dig foxholes, many GIs were drawn from their pits by the sight of aircraft overhead and stood watching the air armada rain devastation on the Germans. US vehicles were massed down each narrow road, nose to tail, and so, when the bombs inexorably began to creep north, there was nothing that the watchers could do but run for cover and pray.

A kilometre north of the crossroads, US bombs hit 3/47th Infantry's battalion command post, wounding the entire command group except for the commanding officer and his executive officer.

To restore momentum, Smythe directed Lt Col Wendel T. Chaffin's 1/47th Infantry to pass through and attack. This resulted in a 90-minute delay, the attack not getting started until 1230 hours.

As the American infantrymen made their way through the gaps in the hedgerows they found that Bayerlein's Panzer Lehr Division, though grievously hurt, could still fight back. At 1300 hours, 1/47th Infantry's leading companies were held up by a roadblock north of the crossroads. Bayerlein defended the D29 with a series of strongpoints and roadblocks based on dug-in and camouflaged Panzer IV and Panther tanks.

It was not until 60th Infantry Regiment advanced along the ridge on the skyline to your west that the Americans began to regain the initiative. Major Max Wolf's 2/60th Infantry was between where you stand and the ridge, on 47th Infantry Regiment's right flank, and 3/60th Infantry was on the skyline, both battalions supported by Sherman tanks and M10 tank destroyers. 3/60th Infantry skirted pockets of paratroopers holding out in le Mesnil-Eury and advanced along the ridge towards the village of Montreuil-sur-Lozon, reaching the outskirts by 1500 hours. Wolf's progress allowed 1/47th Infantry, which had been held up north of where you are standing, to sidestep to the west and finally reach the D900 between the crossroads and le Mesnil-Eury by about 1600 hours. By nightfall 47th Infantry Regiment had fought its way a further kilometre down the D29, but it was still 5 km short of Marigny.

These results disappointed Bradley but Collins at VII Corps sensed that the defences were crumbling. On the night of 25/26 July he unleashed his armour, this crossroads witnessing 3rd Armored Division's CC B pass through, tasked to break through what Collins viewed as the brittle remains of Panzer Lehr's defence.

Stand A2: 25 Juillet 1944 Cobra Monument

DIRECTIONS: Return to the car and drive 3 km further east along the D900. The high ground to the north marks the line of VII Corps' positions for the attack. Stop at the junction with the D189/D89, signposted to la Chapelle-en-Juger and marked by a monument on the south-east of the road, and park in the car park.

THE ACTION: This crossroads was on the boundary of 9th and 4th Infantry Divisions, in the 4th Division area. North of the junction and west of the D189, one can see an area of woodland.

On the right the hedgerows mask a group of buildings, la Cour des Landes, some 300 metres from the junction. Colonel James S. Rodwell's 8th Infantry Regiment attacked along the axis of the road, with 1/8th Infantry on this axis and 3/8th Infantry further to the east. Shermans of 70th Tank Battalion and M10s of C/634th Tank Destroyer Battalion, supported both attacks.

A dead German with his *Panzerschreck* on the road to Marigny, 26 July. *(USNA)*

The area where you stand was defended by what was left of 13th and 14th Paratroop Regiments, under the command of Panzer Lehr Division. Heavy fighting had reduced these two regiments to less than a single battalion's strength when combined. When the attack started the paratroopers were in the process of being relieved by 913th Grenadier Regiment. Even so, 4th Infantry Division faced a series of strongpoints sited north of the D900, covering the routes south, which proved impossible to by-pass. The leading elements of both American battalions soon became involved in clearing positions in the woods to the west of the road and in la Cour des Landes. Infantry–armour cooperation was difficult in such close country and the GIs fighting their way forward had to rely on their bazookas to deal with the German tank strongpoints at close range, while facing intense small-arms fire from the protective ring of panzergrenadiers. Time and time again it was the arrival of armour that dealt with the obstacles and got the advance moving once more. Both battalions fought their way across this road and by 1800 hours had reached the outskirts of la Chapelle-en-Juger.

Then: Private James W. Williamson of Woodside, Ohio, directing traffic in la Chapelle-en-Juger, 27 July. *(USNA)*

Now: Where Private Williamson once stood, a new church includes a memorial to the 'American break-out on our soil'. *(Author)*

Stand A3: La Chapelle-en-Juger

DIRECTIONS: Drive south on the D89 into la Chapelle-en-Juger and park near the church and memorial.

THE ACTION: La Chapelle-en-Juger was in 9th Infantry Division's area and within the bomb zone on 24 and 25 July. By last light on 25 July, elements of 8th Infantry Regiment of 4th Infantry Division were on the northern outskirts of the village, which was subjected to intense artillery fire. On the night of 25/26 July, Collins deployed his armour and the following morning Rodwell's battalions battled for the ruins of la Chapelle-en-Juger. Patrols had probed the village during the night but the crossroads near the church was not secured until morning.

8th Infantry Regiment continued to push south down the D89 against what was left of 353rd Infantry Division. This formation had been tasked with plugging the gap, but after weeks of combat and constant air attacks its five infantry battalions, with companies each numbering fewer than 60 men, were too weak to provide any significant opposition. Suddenly German resistance fell apart as elements of 353rd Infantry Division were overrun and Panzer Lehr Division's artillery was put to flight, and more and more dispirited German defenders surrendered. By nightfall on 26 July, Rodwell had cut the St-Lô–Coutances highway, advancing 6 km in 30 hours.

Stand A4: German Cemetery, Marigny

DIRECTIONS: Head south along the D89, following 8th Infantry Regiment's route. Turn right at the signpost to the German military cemetery at Marigny on the D341. Note the cross at the first farm track on your left and look down the narrow lane between the hedgerows marking the boundaries between two farms. Continue to the entrance to the cemetery, marked by a typical Norman tower, and park in the car park.

THE SITE: After witnessing heavy fighting on 25–27 July 1944, this site was originally a temporary American cemetery where the American Graves Service buried those who were killed in the Cobra battle. In 1945–6 the American dead whose relatives had decided that their bodies should not be repatriated were relocated to the graveyard overlooking Omaha Beach. Next to the car park is a memorial that records this. In 1957 the Reburial Service of the German War Graves Commission relocated the fallen from the many small graveyards and field graves to Marigny, and in 1958 began creating the gardens and buildings at the site.

Stand A5: Marigny Town Square

DIRECTIONS: Continue west along the D341, then turn left on to the D29 to rejoin the route taken by Colonel Boudinot's CC B, 3rd Armored Division, on the road to Marigny. Note the higher ground to the east (left) of the road; here the Germans contested the American advance, with a mix of armour, infantry and self-propelled guns. Drive into the town and park in the car park in the town square immediately past the *Cobra – la Percée* signpost. Walk into the church square. A memorial in front of the church commemorates the 26 townsfolk killed in the Normandy campaign.

GIs move into Marigny town square on 28 July past the junction where the *Cobra – la Percée* sign now stands. German signs indicate the locations of neighbouring units including Battlegroup *Heintz*. (USNA)

THE ACTION: On the night of 25/26 July, CC B was tasked with breaking through Marigny and swinging west towards Coutances. One can imagine the reality of CC B's advance with its reconnaissance elements in front, followed by armour and infantry in half-tracks. The frontage was narrow, 'extending only the distance of one hedgerow to the left and one hedgerow to the

Then: Taking a nap in Marigny, 28 July. *(USNA)*

Now: The modern frontage of the bank which has replaced the seed merchant's where the unknown GI slept. *(Author)*

right of the road', with the Germans who were by-passed closing the gap again and having to be winkled out by the following infantry. However, every telephone pole and all electric, telephone and cable wires were deliberately blasted, shattering German communications and leaving their headquarters unaware of American progress.

The jeeps of Lt Cleveland's Reconnaissance Company, 33rd Armored Regiment, led the way. At each bend in the road, Cleveland brought down artillery fire on the road ahead and then pushed quickly on. Craters from the bombing slowed the advance and a tank-dozer with the recce group was kept busy until knocked out by fire from the strongpoint on the outskirts of Marigny. At this point the leading combat team of tanks and infantry took over.

The route into Marigny was defended by a handful of Panzer IVs and self-propelled guns of 2nd SS Panzer Division, together with grenadiers of 353rd Infantry Division. Both 18th Infantry Regiment and CC B were held on the outskirts at nightfall on 26 July, while reports led Collins to believe the town was taken. It was only on the next day that 18th Infantry Regiment cleared Marigny, street by street, before the remnants of Panzer Lehr Division withdrew.

Stand A6: 30th Infantry Division and the Road to St-Gilles

DIRECTIONS: Retrace your route back up the D29 and continue straight on through Montreuil-sur-Lozon. Turn right at the D900 and drive east. The long straight road that marked the bomb line ends in a large loop to the right as it crosses the River Terrette and climbs up on to the ridge and the junction with the D77. Pass under the new road bridge and take the exit north along the D77. After the first overpass on the new road, stop and park and walk back onto the overpass, which offers a superb view.

THE ACTION: You are now standing overlooking the high ground that was the axis of 30th Infantry Division's attack. The original line of the D77 runs immediately west of the overpass where you stand, and the overpass itself marks the general area of the bomb line on 25 July. The long straight line of the D900 provided the northern boundary of the bomb zone, but here in 30th Infantry Division's area it was marked by coloured artillery smoke. It may be because of this that the division's units suffered some of the worst casualties in the bombing that day.

The division's leading elements had withdrawn about a kilometre north of where you are standing. One can also pick out the line of the D446 E4 where it cuts west to east across the spur. It was here,

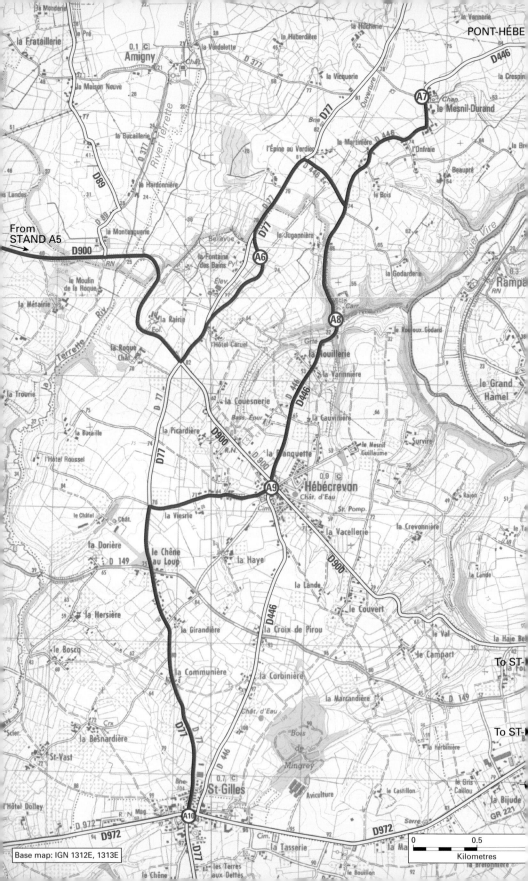

PONT-HÉBE

la Fratellerie

Amigny

From
STAND A5

le Mesnil-Durand

Hébécrevon

St-Gilles

To ST-

To ST-

Base map: IGN 1312E, 1313E

0   0.5

Kilometres

in 2/120th Infantry's area, that Lt Gen Leslie McNair had decided to view the bombing. Having witnessed the abortive bombing the day before, he was determined to share the risk with his men. McNair was reported missing after the bombing hit 2/120th Infantry's headquarters area where he was standing.

Digging out men buried by the bombing, on the high ground north-west of Hébécrevon, 25 July. 2/120th Infantry's attack preparations dissolved into chaos as men frantically dug to free those buried in the blast. *(USNA)*

Colonel Hammond D. Birks' 120th Infantry Regiment was to attack along the line of the ridge down the axis of the D77, break through the German main line of resistance on the Périers–St-Lô highway, seize St-Gilles and allow 2nd Armored Division's CC A to pass through. Birks deployed his troops astride the road in 'column of battalions', spearheaded by 2/120th Infantry, followed in turn by 1/ and 3/120th Infantry.

Lt Col Eads Hardaway's 2/120th Infantry was thrown into confusion but, spurred on by Birks, Hardaway got his men moving at 1130 hours. The battalion was held up by a strongpoint on the former American forward line. This was based on the farm buildings to your west at la Fontaine des Bains. Determined resistance around the farm was only overcome by Shermans of 743rd Tank Battalion, knocking out the Panthers that anchored the German line and then advancing with the infantry. It was a hard fight with heavy casualties: G/120th Infantry lost three commanders in succession. A/743rd Tank Battalion, was stopped by heavy tank and anti-tank fire, losing one Sherman and a platoon commander, Lt David Tickner. The company commander, Lt Ernest Aas, went out on foot and located the German tanks, one of which was then destroyed. At Aas' suggestion, the Shermans moved to the east of the roadblock and engaged five Panthers that were on either side of the St-Gilles road, knocking one out and forcing the others to withdraw, before finally clearing the critical junction on the D900 at nightfall.

While 2/120th Infantry fought its battle Birks deployed Lt Col Cantey's 1/120th Infantry around the left flank to seize the crossroads on the D900 and continue south. The sunken road that marked the crossroads in 1944 (radically changed by modern road building) was strongly defended, but was taken after a deliberate attack. Birks then directed Cantey to seize the crossroads immediately north of le Chêne au Loup on the D77. This involved a night march by tired GIs down the axis of the road, accomplished with little resistance by 0200 hours on 26 July.

Birks also sent 3/120th Infantry to the west of where you are standing. Despite encountering heavy resistance near the D900, by nightfall it had secured the regiment's western flank between la Roque Château and the divisional boundary on the River Terrette.

Stand A7: Le Mesnil-Durand

DIRECTIONS: If possible, drive north along the old D77, and take the first turn to the right, the D466 E4. Turn left at the T-junction on to the D446 and drive towards le Mesnil-Durand along a narrow road. Stop and park outside the church at the junction in the village. (Road works were in progress in this area at the time of writing and their completion may make this route impractical. If so leave the D77 to the east where possible and make your way into le Mesnil-Durand.)

THE ACTION: This was the assembly area for 119th Infantry Regiment's attack on the morning of 25 July. Picture vehicles nose to tail along the road and crammed into every field on either side, together with artillery and all the paraphernalia of war, as they watched the bombing to the south.

Colonel Edwin M. Sutherland's 119th Infantry Regiment was tasked with securing the high ground centred on Hébécrevon, which dominated what is now the D466 to St-Gilles, the planned axis of advance of 2nd Armored Division's CC A. The high ground to the east of Hébécrevon marked the eastern edge of the bombardment zone. Sutherland's plan was to push his regiment in column of battalions down the D466 across the narrow bridge north of la Nouillerie and up into Hébécrevon, with 3/119th leading.

Le Mesnil-Durand church from the D446, showing the memorial to the 'liberateurs' on the wall at the base of the typical Norman church tower. *(Author)*

Stand A8: La Nouillerie Crossing

DIRECTIONS: Drive south down the D466 towards Hébécrevon. Stop at the bridge next to the quarry below la Nouillerie.

THE ACTION: This crossing point, dominated by the high ground ahead, was the site of a roadblock on 25 July. Note the road junction immediately across the stream and the track leading up to your left towards farm buildings at le Rouloux-Godard. You will also see a shrine in a grotto two thirds of the way up the D466 on the right. The defences consisted of three dug-in tanks with infantry, sited on the crest of the ridge above the grotto. German infantry also occupied the farm, and the approach to the crossing was protected by anti-tank and anti-personnel mines. The crossing was also registered as a target by German artillery firing from the high ground east of Hébécrevon.

The tanks of Lt Peter Henderson's 3rd Platoon, Company D,

743rd Tank Battalion (3/D/743rd) led the advance, stopping at the crossing as engineers went forward to clear mines and immediately came under machine-gun fire from the German tanks above the grotto. The leading companies, I and K, of 3/119th Infantry, crossing the stream and deploying on both sides of the road, came under intense machine-gun, mortar and artillery fire. Battlegroup *Kentner*, consisting of 6/ and 7/902nd Grenadiers, held the high ground, with 5/902nd Grenadiers in the farm buildings to the left.

The view from the grotto below la Nouillerie, covering the bridge on the D446 on 119th Infantry Regiment's axis for its attack on Hébécrevon. *(Author)*

Sutherland responded by ordering 1/119th Infantry (Major Robert Herlong), less A Company which was detached, to swing east cross-country and outflank the opposition. Herlong's leading companies crossed the valley to the left of the crossing and hit heavy opposition in the farm at le Rouloux-Godard. The Americans deployed along a hedgerow facing the farm and 'a hot fire fight ensued. Our forces worked up to within hand-grenade distance, and this developed into hand to hand fighting.' Using artillery fire to cover his approach, Herlong pushed a company further east to outflank the farm buildings. This broke the resistance; 50 prisoners were taken, including a company commander, who said that he had been ordered to 'hold the position at all costs'. Herlong pushed on up to the high ground further south but German artillery fire forced his men back into cover to the east of the village.

The crossing remained a bottleneck, with the Shermans of D/743rd Tank Battalion reluctant to move forward. Sutherland told Captain Edward Miller (Assistant Operations Officer, 743rd Tank Battalion), the liaison officer with 119th Infantry Regiment, to establish if there was a tank approach on to the high ground and he went forward on foot. Deciding that, while the roads were impassable, a possible route existed cross-country following 1/119th Infantry, Miller led the way in his tank, but on crossing the stream found that he was alone.

Miller then returned to the junction on foot and found chaos:

'One tank had started to turn the wrong way... Two medium tanks were out of action, one having been hit by an 88 right between the gun and shield, bending the 75 and injuring the bow gunner; the other had flopped off the right side of the road just short of the crossing. The tank that had turned the wrong way, and the tank behind it seemed reluctant to turn, saying that the 88s were zeroed in just beyond the crossing. Capt Miller yelled. "Now listen, by Christ if I can go up there on foot you can take your tanks; you have protection."'

Source: Combat Interviews, 743rd Tank Battalion, 30th Infantry Division, USNA.

One at a time the Shermans followed the route Miller indicated and by nightfall had linked with Herlong's men on the high ground.

Meanwhile, L/119th Infantry, to the west of your location, worked its way around to the flank of the Germans holding the crest line. The fighting went on into the night and it was not until first light on 26 July that 3/119th Infantry reached Hébécrevon.

Stand A9: Hébécrevon

DIRECTIONS: Cross the stream and drive up the D446 towards Hébécrevon. Turn left onto the D900, stop and park.

THE ACTION: At 2130 hours on 25 July, Sutherland ordered Herlong's 1/119th Infantry to seize Hébécrevon. Herlong in turn directed Captain Ross Simmons' A/119th Infantry, which was in the low ground west of the town, to carry out his task.

Look west down the D900 from the stand to the lower ground. This was the approach to the village taken by Simmons' A/119th Infantry which, with C/743rd Tank Battalion, advanced into the village on the night of 25/26 July. There was a roadblock astride the road about 100 metres from where you stand, covered by an anti-tank gun, reportedly an 88-mm, on the south side of the road.

An anti-tank gun and a machine gun opened fire on the column as it approached the roadblock, only to be silenced by tank fire after the Germans made the mistake of setting off a flare to illuminate the tanks on the road. The mines covering the roadblock were removed and Simmons' combat team moved through the now silent village without meeting any further resistance. At 0200 hours, Simmons linked up with the rest of 1/119th Infantry. Sutherland would receive a Silver Star for his regiment's achievements that day.

View from the D900/D446 junction in Hébécrevon, looking west along the approach taken by Captain Simmons' A/119th Infantry. The roadblock was in the area where the road dips into the valley. *(Author)*

Stand A10: St-Gilles

DIRECTIONS: Take the first turning on the right off the D900, which brings you to Hébécrevon church. Turn right and then left skirting around the church. Continue to the junction with the D77, secured by 1/120th Infantry in the early morning of 26 July. Turn left on to the D77 and drive to St-Gilles. On reaching St-Gilles, cross over the D972 and stop and park in front of the church.

THE ACTION: Roadblocks and delay positions were sited down this road. Brig Gen Rose's CC A, 2nd Armored Division, drove out in a long single column along the D77 heading for

St-Gilles and beyond. Rose planned to attack with two battalions up, 2/66th Armor on the right and 3/66th Armor on the left, each accompanied by a company of 22nd Armored Infantry Regiment.

US half-tracks and armour moved down the road:

'As the rapid advance of the armored column was held up at various points, the lead vehicle in each team would shoot off the road and along the border of a field large enough to permit the entire team's vehicles to "leaguer" or coil alongside the hedgerows bordering the field. Germans dug in along the hedgerows were fired on and rooted from their foxholes, and an all-round defense was set up in the square of vehicles. The units would then uncoil as the enemy obstacles to the front had been knocked out or eliminated sufficiently that the column could blast its way through.'

Source: Combat Interviews 259-267, 3rd Armored Division, 27 July – 1 August 1944, USNA.

Some 200 fighter-bombers attacked St-Gilles, but the Germans continued to resist in the face of both aerial bombardment and ground attacks. Rose was impatient to push on and by the afternoon of the 27th CC A was driving past St-Gilles church and down the D77 towards Canisy. The break-through had been achieved.

The tactically important crossroads in the centre of St-Gilles, looking north from the church entrance along the D77. The D77 was the axis of advance of 2nd Armored Division's Combat Command A in the break-out on 26 July. *(Author)*

THIS IS THE END OF TOUR A: St-Gilles is also the start of Tour B. Alternatively St-Lô offers a range of accommodation as does Coutances, and a meditative refreshment in one of the local bistros may be a way to finish a busy day before one drives off.

TOUR B

THE BREAK-OUT: ST-GILLES TO COUTANCES

OBJECTIVE: This tour follows the route taken by Maj Gen Edward H. Brooks' 2nd Armored Division with 22nd Infantry Regiment attached, following CC A as far as Canisy and then concentrating on the exploits of CCs B and R on the general axis of the D38 to Lengronne. The actions of these 2nd Armored Division formations tore open the German defences and ensured that Cobra continued to roll forward in what Maj Gen J. Lawton Collins described as 'some of the wildest mêlées of the war'.

DURATION/SUITABILITY: This tour takes a day. The total distance is some 60 km, all of which can be conducted by car. The route is suitable for those cyclists who may be undeterred by its length; for those with mobility difficulties all points are accessible by car.

APPROACH TO BATTLE: On 25 July, Maj Gen Collins sensed that, despite the slow progress of the attacking divisions of his VII Corps, the German communications and command structure had been damaged more than the attacking troops realised. Collins released his armoured divisions and ordered them to complete the break-through. It was the right decision. Despite the Germans' determined resistance at Marigny, Brig Gen Rose's CC A punched down the D77 and by mid-afternoon was rolling through St-Gilles, opening the exploitation phase of Cobra. Although initially being tasked with erecting a protective fence around Cobra, 2nd Armored Division became the main thrust in VII Corps' pincer movement westwards.

From ST-GILLES

To ST-LÔ

Canisy

B1

D38

Quibou

To
LE MESNIL-HERMAN &
ST-SAMSON-DE-BONFOSSÉ

Carantilly

Dangy

D38

Bois de Dangy

Bois de St-Sauveur

Bois de Soulles

Soulles

B2

le Pont Brocard

River Soulles

le Bourg

D52

Notre-Dame-
de-Cenilly

TAND B4

D38

Kilometres

1   2

Base map: IGN 1313E

Canisy burns as an M8 armoured car of 2nd Armored Division's 82nd Armored Reconnaissance Battalion drives through on the afternoon of 26 July. *(USNA)*

Stand B1: Canisy

DIRECTIONS: Begin at St-Gilles, a few kilometres west of St-Lô on the D972, or which can be reached as the end-point of Tour A. From the St-Gilles crossroads drive south on the D77 towards Canisy. Turn right on to the D38 in the centre of Canisy. Stop and park. Walk back to the junction of the D77 and the D38.

THE ACTION: Canisy was CC A's immediate objective and was overrun in the late afternoon of 26 July before its defenders could react. The German rear areas and headquarters had no inkling that tanks and motorised infantry, supported by fighter-bombers, would range so deep and so quickly behind their lines. Canisy, burning from air attack, was taken after only slight resistance.

From Canisy Rose's armour pushed on south along the D77 in two columns, one heading for St-Samson-de-Bonfossé and the other to le Mesnil-Herman, with the intent of securing the west bank of the River Vire as far south as Tessy-sur-Vire. St-Samson was secured during the night of 26/27 July as was the crossroads immediately north of le Mesnil-Herman. On 27 July, CC A captured le Mesnil-Herman, and took the high ground of Hill 183 2 km to the east even as elements of 2nd Panzer Division were committed west across the Vire to contain the expanding American break-out.

Brig Gen Isaac D. White's CC B followed CC A, moving across the Périers–St-Lô road at midday on 27 July and passing through Canisy three hours later. Initially CC B was to set up blocking positions between Notre-Dame-de-Cenilly and Lengronne, but the delays to 1st Infantry and 3rd Armored Divisions' progress changed that. Collins directed Brooks that CC B should drive all the way to the west coast, becoming VII Corps' main thrust.

Stand B2: Le Pont Brocard

DIRECTIONS: Continue south-west for 12 km down the D38 through Dangy to the tiny hamlet of le Pont Brocard where the D38 crosses the River Soulles. Park near the junction with the D52.

Men of B/41st Armored Infantry manning a 57-mm gun in le Pont Brocard. This gun, commanded by Sergeant James J. Cermak, frustrated German attempts to pass through the town on the night of 27/28 July. *(USNA)*

THE ACTION: Elements of 82rd Armored Reconnaissance Battalion rolled through Dangy on the afternoon of the 27th, creating consternation among German support and artillery units. GenLt Bayerlein of Panzer Lehr Division was holding a meeting at the headquarters of his own and 275th Infantry Division in one of the houses when the Americans drove through and he ended up fleeing cross-country with his staff and soldiers towards le Pont Brocard and Hambye. It led a shocked Bayerlein to report that Panzer Lehr Division was 'finally annihilated'.

Looking west along the D52 from where it links with the D39 in le Pont Brocard. This was Sergeant Cermak's view when he opened fire on the German column attempting to break through the village, 27/28 July. *(Author)*

Pont Brocard was seized late on 27 July by Disney's column. B/41st Armored Infantry was posted to secure the bridge and the roads to the south. A 57-mm anti-tank gun was deployed on the left of the road at the junction where you stand, covering south-east down the D52. On the night of 27/28 July Sergeant James J. Cermak opened fire on a German column moving towards the village from Cerisy-la-Salle. At distances between 50 and 100 metres Cermak engaged motor-cycles and half-tracks, knocking them out one by one in a fight that went on into the early morning. Cermak was awarded the Distinguished Service Cross for this action.

Stand B3: Notre-Dame-de-Cenilly

DIRECTIONS: Drive south on the D38 for 2 km to Notre-Dame-de-Cenilly. Stop in the town square.

THE ACTION: The jeeps, M8 armoured cars, half-tracks and light tanks of 82nd Armored Reconnaissance Battalion and 67th Armored Regiment's Reconnaissance Company roared through

Notre-Dame-de-Cenilly late on the 27th, firing at surprised Germans in the town centre, who desperately sought cover. They were followed by Disney's column, which secured the town and then allowed the left column that was following up to pass through. Disney released a company of tanks and two companies of infantry to hold the town while roadblocks were placed along the routes leading to the D38. The town would become the focus for a series of German counter-attacks attempting to break out to the south-east over the next two nights.

Corporal Buster Sanchez passes out bread from a captured German ration truck at Notre-Dame-de-Cenilly, 29 July. (USNA)

Stand B4: Action at la Pinetière Crossroads

DIRECTIONS: Drive south-west along the D38 for 1.5 km to the first major junction with the D27. This is la Pinetière crossroads, now identified by the large house la Pompe in the north-east corner. Walk west along the D27 to the first junction where a sunken road bounded by high earth banks cuts across.

THE ACTION: CC B, reinforced by the CC R, picketed all the roads leading south on to the D38. Each roadblock in turn was attacked by German columns attempting to break out. Artillery support proved critical to the success of the American defence. This was the task of Lt Col H.M. Exton's 78th Armored Field Artillery Battalion, equipped with M7 self-propelled 105-mm

howitzers, which on the night of 28/29 July was in position around la Pinetière crossroads. Exton's B Battery occupied the field where la Pompe now stands, with C Battery across the D38 in the field at the south-east corner, protected by a 37-mm anti-tank gun sited to fire through the hedgerow at the corner. 1/67th Armor had its headquarters some 500 metres further east down the D27. L/8th Infantry provided immediate protection for the artillery battalion, manning a roadblock 150 metres further west along the D27, with four M10 tank destroyers in support. L/8th Infantry's soft-skinned vehicles were 'harboured up' among the trees north-west of the crossroads.

The crossroads at la Pinetière looking west along the axis of the German attack on the night of 28/29 July from the perspective of the 37-mm gun guarding C Battery, 78th Armored Field Artillery. B Battery was in the area of the hedge and ornamental fence on the right of the road, L/8th Infantry's soft-skinned vehicles were in the trees beyond the building on the left. *(Author)*

78th Armored Field Artillery Battalion had been firing missions all night in support of the various roadblocks. At 0800 hours on 29 July, fire was heard against the roadblock protecting the crossroads. This increased in intensity and it was reported that a German column of 15 tanks and about 200 infantry was attacking from the west down the axis of the D27 towards the crossroads. German mortar fire increased and at 0900 hours the American infantry's soft-skinned vehicles and half-tracks suddenly drove off north-east along the D38 in the direction of Notre-Dame-de-Cenilly. These were followed by three M10 tank destroyers, the fourth having been knocked out, as the infantry defending the roadblock, with their company commander dead, broke and withdrew in panic into B Battery's positions. Exton raced across the road and directed B Battery's six guns into action in the direct fire role. Two already in position, lining the hedgerow marking the sunken road, were joined by the remaining four, which poured fire into the approaching Germans together with machine-gun fire from hastily organised teams of artillerymen. Behind them, C Battery's M7s went into all-round defence as the Germans tried to encircle the position.

A Panzer IV was knocked out 150 metres from the crossroads and a divisional 'stonk', where all available artillery was massed together on a single target, was brought down 500 metres west of the crossroads and repeated three times. About this time that tanks from 1/67th Armor, supported by infantry from 41st Armored Infantry Regiment, arrived and pushed the Germans back up the road towards Roncey. Seven Panzer IVs were knocked out within 1 km of the crossroads and 126 dead German paratroopers were counted. There were no casualties in 78th Armored Field Artillery.

Stand B5: The road to St-Denis-le-Gast

DIRECTIONS: Drive south-west down the D38 through St-Martin-de-Cenilly for 6 km to the junction with the D610, where the D38 bends sharply south to St-Denis-le-Gast. Continue along the D610 for 400 metres to the first crossroads, where the D610 meets the D238. Park near the junction.

The crossroads of the D610 and the D238, looking south towards the fields on either side of the road where 3/67th Armor's headquarters was located on the night of 29/30 July, when it was overrun by the German column. *(Author)*

THE ACTION: The fields on either side of the road south of the junction were the location of the command post of 3/67th Armor (Lt Col Harry L. Hilliard), one of the two battalions of Colonel Sidney R. Hinds' CC R, 2nd Armored Division. Hilliard's command, less I/67th Armor and with F/41st Armored Infantry attached, had moved into position on 29 July, to prevent German attempts to break out from the Roncey area to the north.

Hilliard spent his time visiting his outposts and was away from his command post on the night of 29/30 July, when 2nd SS Panzer Division sent a strong advance guard south down the D238 and parallel roads. At 2300 hours, the weakly-held roadblock north of the command post was overrun and the headquarters area came under heavy fire. Flares, artillery and mortar fire announced the German attack, but things got serious when a Panther started firing over the hedgerow at the crossroads into the mass of headquarters vehicles, setting a half-track on fire. Hilliard could only watch as flares illuminated the night sky and listen as the German attackers 'seemed to be throwing everything in the book at our CP area'.

> **Private William Smith recalled the German attack:**
>
> 'It was the closest hand-to-hand fighting I have ever seen. Some of our boys were machine-gunned and then bayoneted and found the next morning in ditches along the side of the road – always with six or eight Jerries dead around them. About the best example of close-in fighting I remember was when a German rifleman shot Pvt. Small's tommy-gun right out of his hand. Small got mad and beat the Jerry to death with his helmet.'
>
> *Source:* Interview with Private W. Smith, Reconnaissance Platoon, 3/67th Armor, Combat Interviews, USNA.

Vehicles burst into flames as they were hit by tank fire, driving the US defenders to take cover in the surrounding fields while German infantry fought their way through the position and the main German column pushed on south towards St-Denis-le-Gast.

Stand B6: St-Denis-le-Gast

DIRECTIONS: Drive south down the D238, turn right on to the D38 and continue past the cemetery into St-Denis. Turn right on to the D13. Park and walk back to the church at the crossroads.

The crossroads of the D38 with the D13 at the church in St-Denis-le-Gast, looking south. The German column fought its way to this crossroads, driving out the defenders around the church, before turning right and heading west along the D13 towards la Chapelle. *(Author)*

THE ACTION: At about midnight on 29/30 July the German column that overran 3/67th Armor's headquarters continued to fight its way down the D38 into St-Denis-le-Gast. It consisted of approximately 600 men of 2nd SS Panzer and 17th SS Panzergrenadier Divisions and was supported by the bulk of the armour of a panzer battalion, some 90 vehicles of all descriptions. The town was defended by B/41st Armored Infantry with two M10 tank destroyers of C/702nd Tank Destroyer Battalion, and the light tanks of 2/A/67th Armor. There had been fighting all day with small parties of Germans moving through the surrounding countryside. The defenders were warned that a German column had overrun 3/67th Armor's command post and so the light tanks were deployed on either side of the D38 in support of the M10s which covered the northern approach.

A self-propelled 88-mm gun led the column. Infantry overran the graveyard position, forcing the defenders back on the town. Confused fighting broke out around the church and the crossroads. Lt Col Wilson D. Coleman, commanding 2/41st Armored Infantry, personally knocked out one German tank with a bazooka but was later killed. Colonel Hinds made his way into St-Denis-le-Gast to

Inspecting a knocked out Panzer IV, part of the column that drove into St-Denis-le-Gast and was hit by a 37-mm round fired from one of 41st Armored Infantry Regiment's half-tracks immediately west of the church crossroads. A tank crewman is pointing out the entry hole in the skirt protecting the turret. *(USNA)*

assess the situation, only to come under fire and escape in a hail of machine-gun bullets. The defenders were forced out of the town and established hasty roadblocks to the east and south, but the German column turned west in the direction of Lengronne.

When St-Denis-le-Gast was retaken the following morning some 26 vehicles littered the roads, including 7 tanks, and about 130 German dead and 124 wounded were collected. CC R's losses were 13 vehicles and 77 men.

Stand B7: La Chapelle

DIRECTIONS: Drive west along the D13 for 2 km. La Chapelle is a small cluster of houses on the south of the road at the junction with the D102 that is easy to overlook. The triangular intersection of a sunken lane and the D13 and D182 is evident, though the lane itself is closed off by a farmer's electrified fence. Be very careful as off-road parking is limited and the traffic fast.

THE ACTION: By the night of 29/30 July, Exton's 78th Armored Field Artillery Battalion had moved to the fields around la Chapelle. A Battery was deployed to the south and B Battery north of the road. Exton's command post was within Headquarters Battery's area in the triangle of roads south of the D13. There had been skirmishes, with German infantry attempting to break through B Battery's positions around midnight, and at 0215 hours on 30 July two vehicles arrived from St-Denis-le-Gast, reporting the loss of the town. A single M10 tank destroyer, commanded by Sergeant Kenneth Oxenreider, followed. It had been damaged in the fighting but limped along the road into 78th Armored Field Artillery Battalion's area. Behind came a column of vehicles that pulled up on the road between B Battery and Headquarters Battery. Exton's Intelligence Officer, Captain Naubert O. Simard, was interrogating five prisoners by the roadside and immediately identified the vehicles as German.

View of the intersection with the sunken road (hidden by the trees on the right), taken from north of the D13 looking east towards St-Denis. The village of la Chapelle can be seen in the middle distance. A 37-mm gun was sited just left of the sunken road and A Battery to the right as you look at it. Two M7s of A Battery deployed to the area of the gate on the right of the photograph and fired down the road at the nearest German vehicles, some 20 metres away. B Battery, north of the road on the extreme left of the photograph, poured fire into the flanks of the vehicle column on the road. (Author)

Simard ran to Exton shouting a warning, then leapt on to his half-track and fired his .50-calibre machine gun at the leading vehicle, a Panzer IV towing an 88-mm anti-tank gun, at a range of about 20 metres. Exton hurried to the command post and directed the batteries to fire at the vehicles on the road. One of B Battery's M7s nearest to the crossroads fired six rounds into the sides of the line of vehicles and stopped as the command post, only 40 metres away, was in its direct line of fire. Simard's actions prompted all Headquarters Battery's machine guns to open fire and at the same time A Battery moved two of its M7s to fire directly down the road.

Sergeant Oxenreider's M10 had pulled off to the north of the road at the junction of the D102/D13 and had been passed by the entire German column, which ignored the damaged tank destroyer, thinking that it was abandoned. Once the firing started, Oxenreider fired into the rear vehicle, which was an armoured personnel carrier full of infantry.

> **Corporal Edward O'Malley recalled Oxenreider's actions:**
>
> 'We just commenced firing, but they didn't fire back, just continued to yell 'Kamerad'. The first round ignited the personnel carrier, and then we started to fire up the column. We fired a total of 28 rounds… When the 78th started leveling their M7s for direct fire from the front of the column… we had to dismount and move off the road to the north.'
>
> *Source:* Corporal E.T. O'Malley, 2/C/702nd Tank Destroyer Battalion, Combat Interview, USNA.

Disaster had threatened but Simard's actions in firing first swamped the German response. The entire column of 20 vehicles was destroyed. This consisted of two Panzer IVs towing 88-mm guns, two 75-mm self-propelled guns and a mix of half-tracks and soft-skinned vehicles. Forty corpses were counted by the roadside and there were 60 wounded and a further 197 prisoners. Four vehicles were destroyed in 78th Armored Field Artillery Battalion. Five men were killed, including Simard, and another six wounded, including Exton. Captain Simard was awarded a posthumous Distinguished Service Cross for his actions.

Stand B8: Slaughter on the Grimesnil Road

DIRECTIONS: Return along the D13 to St-Denis-le-Gast and turn left on to the D38. Take the left fork on to the D49 at the cemetery. Continue for 5 km, past the turn-off to Grimesnil and over a hill, until you see a memorial on the left at a junction leading to la Chapitre farm. Stop and park. Some 150 metres further on is the junction of the D49 with the D438 to Guéhébert, which leads on to Roncey.

THE SITE: Where you stand was part of a roadblock held by a platoon of Captain W.C. Johnson's I/41st Armored Infantry. Johnson's main position was to the south-east, where the D49 bends over a hill past la Coucourie farm and a sunken road from the south links with it. By the morning of 30 July, the road between le Chapitre and the high ground was jammed solid with burning German vehicles and the air stank with the smell of death. Fittingly this area has long been known as *La Lande des Morts* ('The Region of the Dead') – a name that has passed down through history since a battle between the French and English during the Hundred Years' War when the fields were littered with bodies. That scene was repeated in 1944.

The memorial, 'In memory of the American soldiers and of the civilians killed in "La Lande des Morts" – For Freedom'. This was the location of the roadblock, brushed aside by the attacking German column, which moved nose-to-tail towards the high ground in the distance. *(Author)*

THE ACTION: On the night of 29/30 July a strong German column of infantry and armour moved towards Grimesnil from Roncey. At the junction where you stand Lt Anderson's platoon of I/41st Armored Infantry was deployed, one of a number of US outposts established along the line of the D49. I/41st Armored Infantry's main position was on the high ground to the south-east, where Johnson's headquarters was grouped with that of Captain James R. McCartney's E/67th Armor. That evening McCartney moved with a platoon of tanks to reinforce the infantry platoon outpost where the memorial now stands.

McCartney recalled what happened next:

'About 2320 or 2330, as I was standing by the lead tank, I heard the unmistakably regular "Click, Click, Click" of German infantrymen coming down toward the road junction. I walked to the intersection with my jeep driver, and thinking I saw a vehicle coming down the road I hollered: "Is that a friendly vehicle?" There was no answer. After a few seconds' delay I could hear the doughs [his men] fixing their bayonets and the infantry suddenly opened fire down the road. My lead tank opened up, and then a German self-propelled 75 mm on a Mark IV chassis started firing. With fire coming from three directions, I hit the dirt and then tried to get back to my lead tank without getting hit.'

Source: Captain James R. McCartney, E/67th Armor, After Action Report, USNA.

It was a chaotic situation. McCartney ran back to the first three tanks, directing their platoon commander to 'hold the crossroads for a little while if he could'. German infantry were now infiltrating across the fields and engaging the vehicles on the road with grenades and small-arms fire. The three tanks could not turn around and reversed back up the hill to warn the main position. Finally, with fire coming from either side and with Anderson dead and his platoon dispersed, McCartney ordered his own tank to reverse back, which it did under fire.

On the high ground, McCartney had 20 tanks sited both north and south of the road, with Johnson's armoured infantry dug in round them doing 'a whale of a good job in protecting Company E's tanks from infiltrating bazookamen'. The German column was the main body of both 2nd SS Panzer and 17th SS Panzergrenadier Divisions, led by a high-velocity, self-propelled 75-mm gun. The second vehicle mounted a 150-mm gun, which caused great havoc all evening. Even when not close to this big gun, US personnel felt its concussion. As the column, numbering some 90 vehicles and perhaps 2,500 *Waffen-SS* troops, continued to push forward towards the high ground, McCartney moved his command tank to cover the approach up the road, but it slid into the ditch and had to be abandoned. The first German vehicle was knocked out on the road, 20 metres from the perimeter. Then the slaughter started. From within the perimeter the mortar platoon fired one white phosphorus round for every three of high-explosive; the white phosphorus set

Brig Gen Isaac D. White (on road), commander of CC B, examines destroyed German armour near Grimesnil on 30 July. This photograph was taken on the perimeter of the joint position of I/41st Armored Infantry and E/67th Armor. Close range action knocked out the leading two German vehicles, the second of which was this 150-mm Hummel self-propelled gun, named *Clausewitz*. The second vehicle is a SdKfz 251 half-track bearing the markings of 2nd SS Panzer Division's divisional artillery. It may have been carrying ammunition for the Hummel. Curious GIs ignore its dead crew as they inspect the vehicles. *(USNA)*

fire to the vehicles and lit up the scene, while the high-explosive was particularly effective in destroying German half-tracks.

Tanks of E/67th Armor to the south of the road had excellent fields of fire down the jam-packed column, bringing it to a halt. German infantry continued to infiltrate through the fields on either side but were checked by artillery fire. At times McCartney thought sheer weight of numbers would overrun the position and so all light vehicles and half-tracks were evacuated rearwards.

Facing the main attack up the road, Sergeant Hulon Whittington of I/41st Armored Infantry took over command after his platoon commander went missing and his platoon sergeant was wounded. He arranged to evacuate the wounded, sorted out the defence and when he established that many of his men were pinned down along the line of a hedgerow, 'he rode up to the hedgerow on top of a tank with a number of grenades and proceeded to blast out the enemy almost one by one.' For this action Whittington was awarded the Medal of Honor.

With the flames silhouetting any movement, the German column was bombarded with hand grenades and bazooka rounds. Johnson recalled. 'We stopped them cold and checked their major thrusts… I got a Silver Star out of it… but Hell, I was just there – the other boys did the fighting.' Fire support from 78th Armored Field Artillery Battalion was slowed because the artillery was also under attack at the time (*see Stand B7*). At 0300 hours the artillery fire became effective and the M7s of 62nd and 78th Armored Field Artillery pounded the road between the D438/D49 junction and the hilltop. It was at 0400 hours that the fighting was at its most dangerous, with American infantry and armour beating off repeated infantry attacks. These only ended at daybreak, with a final attempt by infantry to outflank the position north of the road, only to be hunted down by E Company's tanks and killed; some 300 bodies were later counted in the marshy ground.

Stand B9: Roncey

DIRECTIONS: Continue along the D49 for 150 metres, then turn right on to the D438. After 2 km turn left on to the D349, which winds through Guéhébert towards Roncey. Enter Roncey and stop outside the church in the town square.

View of Roncey's town square from the steps of the church, showing the *Cobra – la Percée* signpost, which tells the story of the Roncey pocket. *(Author)*

THE ACTION: The battle of the Roncey pocket was short-lived but violent. Elements of 2nd SS Panzer Division concentrated around the town to bolster the German forces withdrawing from Cerisy-la-Salle and Montpinchon. A huge log-jam of vehicles, weapons and equipment began to build up in the surrounding roads, fields and the town square. This concentration of several hundred vehicles of all kinds was spotted by air reconnaissance. Air and artillery attacks on 28–29 July caused heavy German losses, including over 250 vehicles. Roncey was devastated in these attacks, the church and 46 houses being totally destroyed with a further 43 damaged; six civilians were killed. Many of the buildings that remained were then looted and set on fire by the *Waffen-SS*. The arriving US columns had to bulldoze their way through what remained of the town to clear a way forward.

In the vestibule of the rebuilt church there is a model of the original building; on the wall is a photograph of it after the bombing, surrounded by destroyed vehicles.

A White M3 half-track towing a 37-mm anti-tank gun passes the heaped wrecks of German armour and other vehicles outside the destroyed church in Roncey's town square, 1 August. *(USNA)*

THIS IS THE END OF THE TOUR: To return to Coutances head north-west out of town on the D58.

TOUR C

AVRANCHES: THE DOOR TO BRITTANY

OBJECTIVE: This tour covers the break-out of both VII and VIII Corps from the attritional fighting along the Lessay–Périers–St-Lô line to the fast-moving armoured advance that saw the Americans rapidly capture Coutances and Avranches and, by seizing intact the bridges over the Rivers Sée and Sélune, open the gateway to Brittany.

DURATION/SUITABILITY: A day tour (car with walking), which is suitable for the disabled.

APPROACH TO BATTLE: For Middleton's VIII Corps, July 1944 had been a month of extremes. The attack on the Lessay–Périers sector, 3–15 July, was marked by slow, costly fighting against invariably stubborn hedgerow defence. US casualties were high and gains were measured a field at a time. That all changed on 26 July and, after breaking the defensive crust on 26–27 July, the battle became a rapid advance of armour against what Maj Gen Middleton described as 'a defeated, disorganized and demoralized enemy'. 4th Armored Division's CC B entered Coutances at about 1700 hours on 28 July, where it linked up with elements of VII Corps' 3rd Armored Division. This is commemorated by a memorial to Maj Gen John

Lt Gen George S. Patton surrounded by cheerful Frenchmen near Coutances as he urges VIII Corps forward on 29 July. *(USNA)*

From GRANVILLE

AVRANCHES

To MONT-
DE HUISNES

0		1		2
Kilometres

Base map: IGN 121

S. Wood and 4th Armored Division on the D971 at the entrance to the town.

On 29 July it was obvious that Bradley's First Army had achieved the break-through. VIII Corps was ordered to continue to exploit south along the western part of the Cotentin peninsula and seize Avranches. This attack would be spearheaded by the two armoured divisions, 4th Armored on the left or eastern flank, with 8th Infantry Division following, and 6th Armored on the right or western flank moving in the direction of Granville, along what is now the D971. This tour follows the route of Wood's 4th Armored Division.

Stand C1: Coutances to Pont Gilbert

DIRECTIONS: Drive south from Coutances on the D7 for 32 km. On this route Wood's 4th Armored Division had to squeeze past units of VII Corps and then was delayed by destroyed crossings over the River Sienne. At la Haye-Pesnel turn right on to the D35, continue 7 km to Sartilly and then turn left on to the D973, which is the main road from Granville. This was the route of the columns of 4th Armored Division's CC B. Continue south-east on the D973 and cross the River Sée at Pont Gilbert. Turn right immediately after crossing the bridge and park in the road that leads to the railway station. Walk back to the bridge but be careful of the traffic.

Pont Gilbert over the River Sée in the Marcey-les-Grèves district, looking north-west; here a US company commander lost his nerve and surrendered the bridge to a German column on the night of 30/31 July. *(Author)*

A Sherman tank drives into the centre of Avranches, while in the background the spire of St-Gervais towers over the ruins of the town. *(USNA)*

THE ACTION: VIII Corps' was led by 4th Armored Division. Wood ordered Brig Gen Holmes E. Dager's CC B to capture Avranches and river crossings to the east. German delaying tactics, however, forced the columns to commit dismounted infantry supported by artillery and ground-attack aircraft to clear blocking positions *en route*. Brig Gen Dager personally led the western column, which advanced along what is now the D7 through la Haye-Pesnel and along the D35 to Sartilly.

By late afternoon on 30 July, CC B had taken the road bridges across the Sée at Pont Gilbert and further upriver at Ponts. Dager then pushed forward into Avranches, which sits on dominating high ground, between the Sée to the north and the Sélune to the south. Avranches was a bottleneck; only one major road crosses the River Sélune near Pontaubault, the gateway into Brittany.

While CC B advanced into Avranches, Pont Gilbert was left to be defended by a tank company without infantry support. The US company commander positioned his tanks to protect the bridge and at 2200 hours on 30 July detected a large convoy of German vehicles approaching from the direction of Granville. The leading vehicles were marked with red crosses and were let through across the river. However, troops on the trucks that followed opened fire and the American tanks replied, destroying the vehicles and blocking the road. The German troops, some 300 men, immediately surrendered and the vehicles were found to be carrying ammunition and supplies.

Prisoners revealed that a second column, more heavily armed, was on its way. It arrived at midnight and in the resulting combat an ammunition truck caught fire, illuminating the defenders' tanks around the bridge. The tank company commander, burdened with prisoners, took counsel of his fears and, though he had not lost a man or a tank, ordered a withdrawal to the next bridge up-river, leaving Pont Gibert and the prisoners in German hands.

Between midnight and daybreak German columns passed over the bridge, some heading for Avranches and some heading along the course of the Sée towards Mortain. This tour follows those who moved into the city on the hill.

Stand C2: Avranches

DIRECTIONS: Turn right on to the D973 and follow the signs up the Rue du Tertre de la Gare into the centre of Avranches. Park in the Place Valhubert near the information centre; from here a short walk along the Rue d'Islande leads to the castle keep, which offers a brilliant panorama over the northern approaches to the town.

THE ACTION: The situation in Avranches was chaotic in the early hours of 31 July. Dager's elements of CC B suddenly found themselves under attack from Germans pushing into the town from the north. The Germans made two attempts to break out to the south of Avranches, each being driven back after fierce fighting. Private William H. Whitson was awarded a posthumous Distinguished Service Cross for using his machine gun to destroy nearly 20 soft-skinned vehicles and kill some 50 Germans before he himself was killed.

Once Dager discovered that Pont Gilbert had been abandoned, he ordered the tank company to retake it. By this time CC A, also now under Dager's command, had linked up and assisted CC B in securing Avranches by engaging German artillery that had been positioned on the bluffs overlooking the river crossings from the south.

Stand C3: The Patton Memorial

DIRECTIONS: Drive out of the square along the Rue du Dr Gilbert and left along the Boulevard Maréchal Foch, which leads to the Place Patton. Park and walk to the memorial.

The memorial to 'la glorieuse armée Americaine du Général Patton' in Avranches' Place Patton, flanked on one side by an M4 Sherman tank and on the other by a *Voie de la Liberté* milestone, one of the series which marks the route taken by American forces in their battle to liberate France. The soil and the trees around the memorial were brought from the United States. (*Author*)

THE ACTION: By nightfall on 31 July, 4th Armored Division had secured Avranches and at Patton's direction was pushing south to capture the critical Sélune crossings. Patton's eyes were fixed on Brittany and his aim was to get his armour across the Sélune as quickly as possible.

Stand C4: Musée de la Seconde Guerre Mondiale

DIRECTIONS: Drive south down the D7 from Place Patton and out of town. Turn right at the major roundabout under the N175 *autoroute* and then right again, following the signs to the museum.

Avranches World War II Museum

Musée de la Seconde Guerre Mondiale, le Val-Saint-Père, 50300 Avranches; tel: +33 (0)2 33 68 35 83. Admission charge.

BATTLEFIELD TOURS

German prisoners march into captivity near Avranches, August 1944. *(USNA)*

THE SITE: The museum has a major collection of uniforms and equipment of both Allied and Axis forces relating to the Second World War. It has a rare surviving example of one of the Rhino ploughs made from Normandy beach obstacles and mounted on M4 Sherman tanks to assist in the break-out from the *bocage*.

Stand C5: Pontaubault Bridge

DIRECTIONS: From the museum drive south along the D43E for 2 km until it passes over the bridge across the Sélune at Pontaubault. Park on the southern bank of the river and walk back to the bridge.

THE ACTION: The bridge has a description at the southern end describing its importance during the French Revolution and its seizure by the American forces on 31 July 1944. Dager directed CC A, 4th Armored Division, to seize the bridge, the second crossing at Ducey and two nearby dams. Colonel Bruce C. Clarke divided his command into four task forces and directed them to his four targets. All were achieved with little opposition from enemy forces that were still surprised at the speed of the

The bridge over the Sélune at Pontaubault, looking inland from the south bank; its capture allowed Patton's seven divisions to race into Brittany and confirm the destruction of the German defence of Normandy. *(Author)*

American advance. CC A secured the main bridge on the late afternoon of 31 July as well as the road junction south of the village. A German force was moving towards the bridge at the same time and was dispersed by tank and artillery fire.

By the afternoon of 1 August, Wood's 4th Armored Division was rolling over the Pontaubault bridge and by early evening it was deep into Brittany. Patton was up front, seeing to progress and jumping in when things were not happening as fast as he wanted.

> **When he found traffic hopelessly snarled in Avranches 'Patton the commanding general became Patton the efficient traffic cop'. Drivers found themselves being directed by 'none other than Patton himself':**
>
> 'Every manual of road movement was ground into dust. He and his staff did what the whole world knew couldn't be done: it was flat impossible to put a whole army out on a narrow two-lane road and move it at high speed. Everything was going to come to a screeching halt. He even intermingled units. Yet out of the other end of the straw came divisions ready to fight. If anybody else could have done it, no one ever got that man's name.'
>
> *Source:* General Omar Bradley, quoted in Carlo D'Este, *A Genius for War*, p. 627.

THIS IS THE END OF THE TOUR: Regardless of how much is left of the day, a drive to the coast overlooking Mont-St-Michel replicates the experience of Third Army as it raced into Brittany. On the way it is also possible to visit the Mont d'Huisnes German Military Cemetery. Continue south on the D43E until it meets the D43 at a major intersection. Turn right and follow the D43 to the coast where it meets the D75, then follow the D75 until the signposted turn-off on the right. The cemetery holds the remains of 11,956 German personnel. It stands on a 30-metre high hill and a high concrete cross set in the centre of a grassed courtyard towers over it.

GIs stop to view Mont-St-Michel, *en route* to the Brittany ports, 6 August. *(USNA)*

TOUR D

MORTAIN ATTACK: THE NORTHERN THRUST

OBJECTIVE: A tour looking at how the main German thrust west along the axis of the River Sée in Operation *Lüttich* was met and eventually defeated by Collins' VII Corps over the period 7–12 August 1944, with particular emphasis on the crucial role of 117th Infantry Regiment in and around St-Barthélemy.

BATTLEFIELD TOURS

DURATION/SUITABILITY: A half-day tour, mainly conducted by car but with some walking, that may be difficult in places for the disabled. For those with less time, Tours D and E can be combined into a single-day car tour.

APPROACH TO BATTLE: Operation *Lüttich* was aimed at strangling the American logistical lifeline in the Avranches bottleneck. The D5 was the axis of the attack; a network of minor roads in the river valleys nearby followed the same path, but it was the high ground along the course of the D5 that was central to German planning. The attack along *Lüttich*'s northern axis would be spearheaded by 2nd Panzer Division, advancing in two columns south of the River Sée, with 116th Panzer Division advancing north of the river. 2nd Panzer Division's southern column, led by 2nd Panzergrenadier Regiment with elements of 3rd Panzer Regiment, was to attack along the D5.

On the night of 5/6 August, 30th Infantry Division moved from Tessy-sur-Vire to relieve 1st Infantry Division in the Mortain area. As part of this move, 117th Infantry Regiment relieved 26th Infantry Regiment, covering the northern boundary with 9th Infantry Division: 1/117th Infantry was positioned in St-Barthélemy and 3/117th Infantry on the ridge overlooking Bellefontaine.

Like the other elements of 30th Infantry Division, Lt Col Walter M. Johnson's 117th Infantry Regiment was now a veteran unit, but it took over a position that had been sited to meet the needs of an ongoing advance and not those of defence. The field telephone lines that the regiment inherited had been laid in haste and would not meet the demands placed upon them in the days to come.

Stand D1: St-Barthélemy

DIRECTIONS: From the Place Patton roundabout in Avranches, take the northern exit by the police station and turn right at the first set of lights on to the D5 (Rue de Mortain/Rue du Commandant Bindel), heading east to Mortain. An early start may well allow you to experience the morning mists that often cover the river flats and seep up onto the high ground. It was this mist that hid the German armoured columns until about mid-morning as they pushed west on 7 August 1944. Continue east along the D5 and through Juvigny-le-Tertre, until you reach St-Barthélemy. Park at the *mairie* (town hall) opposite the war memorial.

② Elements B/117th Infantry
③ Forward Headquarters 1/117th Infantry,
   A/ and C/117th Infantry
④ Observation post, C/117th Infantry
⑤ German attack
   Base map: IGN 1415O

le Château

Langotière

la Sablonnière

D 79

St Barthélemy

259

D 79

0,4 C

307

Chât. d'eau

Cim.

D5

To MORTAIN

256

③

D2

293

le Bois du Parc

D1

Éc.

280

⑤

D 33

D33

298

la Rousselière

④

⑤

266

D5

la Cervellière

269

la Touvrablère

D279

256

D4

le Pas

287

la Foutelaye

la Tourablère de Haut

la Tourablère

D33

②

la Chaumondière

291

le Domaine

le Gué

les Rouillères

Fout'an Comu

la Haut

D5

la Tourablère de Haut

D5

la Rossaye

From JUVIGNY-LE-TERTRE

①

THE ACTION: The *mairie* was the tactical headquarters of Lt Col Robert E. Frankland's 1/117th Infantry. The battle of the US left (northern) flank along the line of the River Sée is very much the story of Frankland's defence of St-Barthélemy and his fighting withdrawal and continued resistance beyond the village. Frankland had served in the National Guard for almost 20 years; the hard core of his battalion was made up of men he had known and trained with back in Tennessee and he regarded 1/117th Infantry as his personal property.

117th Infantry Regiment found itself having to dig in with only road maps of the area for reference; the requested detailed maps had not yet arrived and so the coming battle would be fought with only a hazy notion of exact locations. Also, little was known about friendly positions; 9th Infantry Division's 39th Infantry Regiment was known to be north of the river, but no link-up was made across the northern divisional boundary. Frankland had been told that there were Germans to the north-east and this became his defensive focus. Elements of three German divisions, including 2nd Panzer Division, were known to be north of Cherencé-le-Roussel. The Americans believed that in the unlikely event of a German counter-attack, the weight of it would fall on 9th Infantry Division.

Frankland had three companies available, plus part of the regimental anti-tank company. A/117th Infantry covered the northern flank in an arc stretching from the D5 in the direction of Juvigny-le-Tertre across to the D33 to the north-west and then in an arc covering the church and cemetery to include what is today the D79 from the crossroads with the D977 at la Tournerie. The company also established a 'rather weak outpost manned by a few riflemen and a bazooka team' at the la Sablonnière road junction to the south-east. C/117th Infantry covered the eastern and southern approaches in an arc including the section of the D5 that ran south-east to join the D977, and also a farm track to the east that linked up with the D977 at la Sablonnière farm. C/117th Infantry's roadblock at the junction of the D5 and D977 was weak, however. Frankland's deployment of Companies A and C reflected the assessment that little threat was expected from the direction of Mortain. Company B was positioned 500 metres west of the village, with a roadblock at the D279/D33 junction to the north-west.

Attached to 1/117th Infantry were six towed 3-inch anti-tank guns of 2nd and 3rd Platoons of Captain Francis Wilts' B/823rd Tank Destroyer Battalion. Although delayed by sporadic artillery

		HQ, 117th Infantry Regiment
②		Rear HQ, 1/117th Infantry
③		Forward HQ, 1/117th Infantry
④		HQ, A/117th Infantry
⑤		HQ, B/117th Infantry
⑥		HQ, C/117th Infantry
⑦		1st Platoon, A/117th Infantry
⑧		2nd Platoon, A/117th Infantry
⑨		3rd Platoon, A/117th Infantry
⑩		2nd Platoon, B/117th Infantry
⑪		3rd Platoon, B/117th Infantry
⑫		1st Platoon, C/117th Infantry
⑬		2nd Platoon, C/117th Infantry
⑭		3rd Platoon, C/117th Infantry

Base map:
GSGS 4347 Mortain 34/10NE

le Bois du Parc

St Barthélmy

la Sablonnie

le Fantay

la Fouelaye

Hubercière

la Rossaye

la Tourablère

la Pourcerie

3-inch anti-tank gun

57-mm anti-tank gun

Road-block

German attacks

Metres
0   250   500

and mortar fire, the guns were in position by 0300 hours on 7 August, at which time St-Barthélemy 'was as quiet as a graveyard', according to Wilts. In 117th Infantry Regiment, as in the rest of 30th Infantry Division, 'no one sensed the coming storm'.

At 0600 hours the German attack started with an armoured thrust on all the routes into the village. By telephone, Frankland instructed his two forward companies to stay in place, let the tanks move through to be engaged by the anti-tank guns, and concentrate on engaging the infantry that would follow. With the situation becoming critical Frankland then rang the regimental command post, at la Rossaye just over 1 km to the west, and asked for help, but Lt Col Johnson could only release a section of two 3-inch anti-tank guns of Lt Lawson Neel's 1/B/823rd Tank Destroyer Battalion.

Frankland's positioning of his battalion was a model of its kind and showed how much the unit had gained in tactical skill during the Normandy fighting. He later said that 'it was a mistake trying to hold with 2 companies' and that 'if he'd realized the strength of the attack he'd have withdrawn and fought a delaying action until they could have counter-attacked or held with greater force'. The attacking armour 'made short work of our AT and TD guns astride the road, although our guns and bazookas got many of them'. (Combat Interviews 95-97, 30th Infantry Division, 6-12 August 1944, USNA.) However, although the strength of the attack caught the defenders by surprise, the battalion achieved a great deal in its dogged defence of the village.

One of Lt Neel's 3-inch guns got into position opposite the battalion command post, ready for the German armour coming in from the east, as Neel recalled:

'The gun in town gave very effective aid for a while. Private [Robert] Dunham killed a tank commander who was leading the tank afoot, and the crew then got the tank with the TD (anti-tank gun). The crew was under unusually heavy small arms fire. Two of the crew's NCOs were wounded by rifle grenades. A second tank approached the position, but no ammunition was at hand. Private T.L. Smith volunteered to cross the street to the half track to replenish the supply, which he did under MG fire. Two other men followed, but couldn't come back due to heavy fire. When the ammunition was finally obtained the gun could not fire on the tank as the gun was in such a position just to the side of a house that a post prevented it from firing... and a Jerry tank knocked it out. Lieutenant Neel consequently ordered his men to withdraw. [As they moved back] Private [Milton] Daly [was so concerned that he] cried "This ain't running away, is it, Lieutenant? This ain't running away, is it?"'

Source: Combat Interviews 93-97, 30th Infantry Division, 6–12 August 1944, USNA.

There were so many tanks coming in from every direction that, despite being held up on the southern axis, others pushed on straight into the village and caught the battalion command group unawares. The Operations Officer, Captain David Easlick, saw armour pull up in front of the headquarters building and at the same time noises were heard to the rear. When Frankland investigated he saw two signallers being marched off with their hands up. A crack pistol shot, Frankland shot the two Germans who had captured his men.

The war memorials and parking area opposite the *mairie* in St-Barthélemy. It was here that German armour pulled up outside Frankland's advanced headquarters, forcing him and his staff to bail out of the windows and rapidly withdraw to join A/117th Infantry, in the area of the line of buildings in the background. *(Author)*

Frankland then raced across to A/117th Infantry's command post to contact Johnson for reinforcements, while Easlick and the rest of the command group made their way to B/117th Infantry's command post, ordering the company commander, Captain Fredolph Hendrickson, to swing his platoons round to meet the threat from the centre of the village. A/117th Infantry's command post had been overrun, so Frankland directed what was left of the company to pull back to Hendrickson's positions and briefed Johnson from there. Easlick also ordered the battalion transport, parked on the outskirts of the village, to withdraw towards Juvigny. This it did, running a gauntlet of tank and machine-gun fire.

Lt Neel's party also withdrew, making their way back to their second gun, at the crossroads immediately east of the regimental headquarters. It became the focus of the next defensive line.

Stand D2: St-Barthélemy – C Company's Battle

DIRECTIONS: Walk to the D5/D33 crossroads.

THE ACTION: This was the centre of Captain Walter Schoener's C/117th Infantry's position, with 1st Platoon to the right of the road looking south-east and 2nd Platoon on the left. Two 3-inch guns from Lt George Greene's 3/B/823rd Tank Destroyer Battalion, were sited on either side of the crossroads and covered the south-east approach along the D5. An observation post was further down the road on the high ground to the left and three 57-mm anti-tank guns were sited in the lower ground on the other side of the road to fire on vehicles advancing along the D5 from the south-east. The men had dug two-man foxholes and occupied positions that allowed them to cover the tracks and roads into the position and also the fields in between. The hedgerows made it difficult to get good fields of fire, both for 1/117th Infantry's own 57-mm anti-tank guns and for Greene's guns. On the left flank next to the church 3rd Platoon covered both the D79 and the farm track that ran towards la Sablonnière.

At about 0600 hours, A/117th Infantry's roadblock to the east at la Sablonnière was overrun. Frankland immediately called in artillery fire on the junction where the farm entrance meets the D977, but communication problems meant that no fire support came. C/117th's roadblock to the south was then broken also, and German tank columns accompanied by infantry drove into the village. Panthers from 1st SS Panzer Regiment advanced along the D5 while Panzer IVs from 3rd Panzer Regiment moved in along the D79 and up the track from la Sablonnière. 1st SS Panzer Regiment was following up 2nd Panzer Division's leading elements, but had caught up and by chance moved into the village from the south, thinking it had already been cleared.

It was a chaotic situation in a thick fog that made it difficult to pick friend from enemy. Vehicles or figures loomed out of the murk at little more than 10 or 20 metres, rifles and machine guns fired in every direction and every squad was engaged.

Private First Class Alfred Overbeck of C/117th Infantry recalled:

'They came out of a wall of fog. I don't know what kind they were. They were so big, they looked like battleships. They were bumper to bumper. The attack was altogether unexpected. They took us entirely by surprise.'

Source: Alwyn Featherston, *Saving the Breakout*, p. 96.

A view along the D5, from the perspective of the German armour driving into town. 3-inch guns were positioned at the D5/D33 junction on either side of the modern two-storey building in the middle distance, which is the location of Stand D2. From this viewpoint, C/117th Infantry's 1st Platoon was on the left of the road and 2nd Platoon was on the right. The leading Panther of 1st SS Panzer Regiment was knocked out at the point from which this photo was taken; it took an hour for the attackers to move it out the way. *(Author)*

About eight German tanks drove along the track from la Sablonnière farm and along the D79 from the north-east into the village past 2nd and 3rd Platoon's positions, peppering the infantry foxholes with machine-gun fire as they passed. The anti-tank guns fired at the tank's gun flashes; Corporal Chester J. Christianson's No. 1 gun of Greene's platoon, sited on the northern side of the crossroads, knocked out the leading Panther advancing from the south-east on the D5. This held up the attackers on this route for nearly an hour, but the panzergrenadiers kept probing forward. When the Panthers advanced again Christianson held his fire and disabled a second some 30 metres from the junction, setting it on fire. Privates Antonio Barrias and George Schiler got another with five rounds from a bazooka at close range. But the tanks kept coming, with their accompanying panzergrenadiers subjecting the gun crews to heavy small-arms fire. One by one the American guns were knocked out and the crews killed or captured. The bazookas proved their worth in this close-quarter fighting, however, where GIs engaged armour flank-on at point-blank range.

2nd and 3rd Platoons were now surrounded; tanks sprayed their positions with machine-gun fire, and most surrendered after a short fight. Led by their NCOs, some 13 men of 2nd Platoon fought their way out and headed back towards the rear, where they linked up with the battalion over the following days. Individual wars were fought by privates like Pete Preslipsky of 3rd Platoon, manning one of the forward observation posts covering the la Sablonnière track, who had already earned the Distinguished Service Cross for destroying a dug-in tank on 12 July. Finding his bazooka would not work, Preslipsky withdrew, picked up an abandoned bazooka and with two rounds accounted for two tanks by putting a rocket into the engine area of each at close range, before pulling back.

Company C's 1st Platoon, on the south side of the D5, also found itself being by-passed. Its men fought a delaying withdrawal from hedgerow to hedgerow while the company command post in the rear was overrun and Captain Schoener and his staff taken prisoner. The withdrawing elements linked up with 1st Platoon, Company B, under Sergeant J.A.W. Parks, who had been directed by Frankland to move forward and assist in Company C's defence. Under the command of Lt Quentin W. Robb, commander of Company C's Weapons Platoon, both platoons held part of a sunken track running south from the junction of the D5/D33 at the southern edge of the village for some two hours, firing at any attempt by the panzergrenadiers to 'pepper-pot' forward by fire and movement.

By 1000 hours, P-47 Thunderbolts were overhead, strafing the German columns, and Robb placed marker panels to designate the GIs' lonely and increasingly untenable position. A messenger was sent to regiment for orders but was not heard from again. At about 1030 hours, Robb sent his men back in four columns towards the regimental command post; during this move, Private Camela Stillatano kept 'knocking out' machine guns with his bazooka. Once again it was the NCOs who held the squads together, Sergeant Parks doing a 'wonderful job' keeping his men in cover, withdrawing each group slowly and calmly, and stopping 'them from running and being spotted'. (Combat Interviews, 95-97, 30th Infantry Division, 6-12 August 1944, USNA.)

Stand D3: St-Barthélemy – A Company's Battle

DIRECTIONS: Walk from the D5/D33 junction north towards the church and then a little way north-west along the D33.

The view from the 3rd Platoon, Company C, position astride the la Sablonnière track, looking towards the 3rd Platoon, Company A, position astride the bend on the D79. Apart from the sealed roads, this area would have had a similar feel in August 1944. *(Author)*

THE ACTION: From here you can see the fields of fire and observation available to A/117th Infantry. Lt Myrl N. MacArthur had been in command of Company A for a week; of his 135 men, 55 were green replacements who had arrived over the previous two days. MacArthur's three platoons were sited on the edge of the village in an arc along the ridge overlooking the valley to the north. Although covering a wide area, this was potentially a strong position, with good fields of fire over the lower ground and routes into village. The increasing noise of tank movement and artillery fire meant that, by 0430 hours on 7 August, everyone in A/117th Infantry was awake.

A view to the east from outside the church at St-Barthélemy towards where the farm track from la Sablonnière links to the D79, then also a farm track, which then contours down in a wide loop into the river valley. 3rd Platoon, Company C's position was astride the farm track on the higher ground. It was linked in with Company A's 3rd Platoon position, which covered the approach along the D79 and was located beyond the bend in the middle distance. This position was untenable once German armour and infantry overran the 3rd Platoon, Company C position on the higher ground. *(Author)*

At 0600 hours, armour from 3rd Panzer Regiment trundled into village from the north-west, down the D33. As the American survivors recalled, 'It was very foggy, however, and it was difficult to see them until they were practically upon us.' Company A found itself attacked by tanks and infantry from the north-west and up the tracks from the east and north-east. Sergeant Carl Brizidine's 3rd Platoon, covering the farm tracks leading into the village from the north-east on what is now the D79, was attacked by armour from the rear. In the fight that followed five men managed to withdraw into the lower ground to the north and loop round towards B/117th Infantry; the remainder were killed, wounded or captured. The men of 2nd Platoon, in the area of the church and cemetery, were swiftly overrun and captured, as were MacArthur and his headquarters staff. Only 1st Platoon managed to extricate itself in any strength and fight its way back towards Company B's positions. At the end of four days' fighting, Company A would have an effective strength of one officer and about 15 men.

Stand D4: La Cervellière – B Company's Battle

DIRECTIONS: Walk back to the *mairie* in St-Barthélemy. Drive north-west along the D5 towards Juvigny. After 800 metres take the second turning to the right, which is a narrow turnoff on the prominent bend in the road as it loops to the left towards Juvigny. Drive along the narrow road for some 300 metres and park in the area of the junction of the two farm tracks. This is la Cervellière, which was known as 'le Fantay' on 1944 maps, presumably a corruption of 'le Foutai Canu', which is how it is marked on today's IGN map. In some accounts it is also referred to as the 'la Foutelaye position', from the name of another nearby hamlet. Where you are parked was the centre of B/117th Infantry's position. Now a maze of buildings among the trees, in 1944 it was an orchard. Walk along the track to the north-east down the steep slope to the crossroads, where the track meets the D33 and then becomes the D279.

The position of the B/117th Infantry roadblock, looking north across the D33 along the D279. German tanks bumped the roadblock at midnight on 6/7 August, knocking out one of Lt Cushman's 57-mm guns and forcing his men to pull back up the track from which this photo was taken. Attempts to re-establish the roadblock failed and the group took up a position halfway up the hill. *(Author)*

THE ACTION: This D279/D33 junction was the position of Lt Robert Cushman's roadblock on the night of 6/7 August. His force comprised two 57-mm anti-tank guns from the battalion's anti-tank platoon, covering the approach from the north, backed up by two heavy machine guns and a squad from 3rd Platoon, Company B. German tanks had probed the entrance to the track at this crossroads earlier in the evening of the 6th, but at midnight they advanced up the track, with panzergrenadiers on either flank. One of the anti-tank guns opened fire on the leading tank, hitting it but doing no damage against its heavy frontal armour. It returned fire, killing and wounding the crew and causing Cushman to pull his men back. Frankland ordered the roadblock to be re-established but artillery fire wounded some of the squad as they made their way forward. Now reluctant to move, they took up a position half-way down the hill astride the track.

The rest of Captain Hendrickson's command was positioned on the high ground in a north-facing arc from north-west to north-east, contouring around the lip of the ridge overlooking the D33. Once the German attack began Hendrickson, on Frankland's instructions, deployed his 1st Platoon forward. With B/117th Infantry under increasing pressure from tanks and infantry fighting their way up the slopes, Frankland 'realized the futility of holding this position and hoped to extricate what was left to a better line, reorganize and hold.' At 0830 hours he withdrew B/117th Infantry back to the crossroads immediately east of the regimental headquarters position, while attempting to contact and pull back Companies A and C.

With chaos all around, not all of Company B's men managed to withdraw. Six men from 2nd Platoon stayed put in their foxholes as an RAF Typhoon attack drove the German infantry to ground and smashed into the armour attempting to move west along the D5. Fearing air attack, the GIs formed the letters 'U.S.' with their raincoats to let the RAF pilots know who was downstairs. The six men stayed put all day, finally pulling out at 1700 hours and making their way back to the regimental headquarters area. Small groups or individuals filtered in over the next two or three days, but the battalion still mustered less than a full strength infantry company.

Stand D5: La Rossaye – The Last Stand

DIRECTIONS: Drive west along the track to the junction with the D5. Turn right and drive west 600 metres to the signposted parking area marked by the blue farm cart at the entrance to la Rossaye, and park. 117th Infantry Regiment's headquarters was established in a farmhouse at la Rossaye south of the D5. Walk 250 metres back along the road towards St-Barthélemy to the junction of the road on the right going south to la Tourablère.

Looking east past the blue farm cart which marks the parking area and the entrance to the farm buildings at la Rossaye. This was the location of the regimental headquarters of 117th Infantry Regiment throughout the battle for St-Barthélemy. The regimental command post became known as 'Château de la Nebelwerfer' as every square metre around the house and farm buildings seemed to be hit, but the house itself was untouched. *(Author)*

THE ACTION: Here, astride the main road and covering the track to the north and south, Frankland built up his defensive line with everything he could salvage of his battalion. As you can see, the track bisects the main road at a point where the ridge falls away on both flanks, offering good fields of fire. It was against this line that the German armoured column advanced through St-Barthélemy and along the D5 towards Juvigny.

Frankland built up his position with Company B and then as the day progressed with some 25 men of Company A and 55 of Company C as the remnants of these companies fought their way back. He was reinforced by everything that Johnson could give him. Just forward of this point Lt Neel engaged German armour with his No. 2 gun, from behind a hedgerow covering the bend. The first shot stopped the leading tank in the middle of the road;

its crew hastily abandoned it, and it stood there with its engine running. Two more tanks followed it up. For some 45 minutes Neel's gun team waited as the two tanks edged forward. Finally the aimer, Private Raymond Dautrieve, knocked out the first of the two and blocked the road. The second tank fired, wounding Dautrieve and also Sergeant Joseph Pesak, the gun commander.

Neel pulled the gun team back and stumbled on the line of infantry digging in behind him. 'Cooks, clerks, messengers and truck drivers' from the Regimental Headquarters Company were thrown in to support what was left of 1/117th Infantry. Frankland held the line with B/117th to the north and what was left of A/ and C/117th to the south. During the afternoon of 7 August Company B was pushed forward to give more depth, but here and on subsequent days, any US advance was limited by the difficulties of hedgerow fighting.

The sun soon burned off the morning mist and by midday RAF Typhoons were overhead looking for targets. Between the aircraft, 823rd Tank Destroyer Battalion's anti-tank guns and the infantry's bazookas, some 30 German vehicles were knocked out or abandoned that afternoon, many of them piling up on the curve in the road and forming an effective roadblock. The casualties inflicted on the German infantry in the fight for the village now proved decisive. The hedgerows presented the same difficulties to the Germans in the attack as they had to the Americans. The weakened US defensive line held because the initial German attacks were poorly co-ordinated; the lack of infantry protection left the panzers isolated and vulnerable to short-range bazooka fire, while the panzergrenadiers were committed without armoured support.

As the day progressed, 1/117th Infantry came under intense artillery and mortar fire. Veterans remembered it as the 'heaviest concentration of artillery they had ever experienced. The Germans fired everything from 88s to 170s and included the regimental CP in their targets.' (Combat Interviews 95-97, 30th Infantry Division, 6–12 August 1944, USNA.) Johnson's command post was now less than 400 metres from the front line but he stayed put, aware that any withdrawal by his headquarters would impact on his men.

The fighting continued over the following days; it was hard gritty work, 'winning a hedgerow a day'. On the morning of 8 August, for example, the German infantry attacked before the mists lifted, coming through the hedgerows against B/117th Infantry, but the attack failed.

Lieutenant G.E. Thompson at I/117th Infantry's command post, immediately behind the front lines in the fight for St-Barthélemy, on 11 August. *(USNA)*

Captain Fredolph Hendrickson recalled:

'They had American M-1s, trench knives, even [US] field jackets (a few days later they were seen wearing our helmets), and a close fight followed for about 30 minutes. There was hand to hand fighting, even fist fights. One Jerry jumped over the hedge and into a foxhole with an American aid man, asked if he were armed and when he saw that the medic was wounded he apologized, got out of the hole and went about his business of finding some other doughboy.'
Source: After Action Reports, 117th Infantry Regiment, USNA.

On 12 August, as the Germans finally pulled back, the GIs pushed forward into the smoking ruins of what had been St-Barthélemy. Lt Col Johnson and Major Warren Giles of the regimental staff were among the first Americans to re-enter the village.

Giles described the village as a heap of smoking rubble:

'That little town – and it was just a small town, really – was totally destroyed. I don't know if there was anything left standing. There were German bodies everywhere. And tanks... a world of burnt out tanks.'

Source: After Action Reports, 117th Infantry Regiment, USNA.

On 6 August, 1/117th Infantry had numbered 28 officers and

The church at St-Barthélemy, like the town, was destroyed in the August fighting, and has been rebuilt on the ruins. A memorial window commemorates the townsfolk who were killed during the war. *(Author)*

600 enlisted men; casualties during the fighting amounted to 7 officers and 352 enlisted men. The skill with which Lt Col Frankland had sited his companies is evident. After the battle he agonised over his actions, but the stand made by his forward two companies and the attached anti-tank guns inflicted casualties that the German infantry and armour could not afford; it also imposed sufficient delay for the morning mists to clear and for the tank columns to come under fighter-bomber attack. One can surmise how more effective the defence would have been with another day's preparation and with the appropriate maps being issued but, even so, it was a gem of a position. The depth position outside the village then became a choke-point that held the German armour in place.

Frankland's stand was as important as 2/120th Infantry's more famous battle on the heights above Mortain (*see Tour E*). Maj Gen Hobbs believed that 1/117th Infantry, by holding the German infantry at St-Barthélemy and then the armour at la Rossaye, saved 30th Infantry Division from disaster.

THIS IS THE END OF THE TOUR: Continue east along the D5 to return to Avranches.

TOUR E

MORTAIN ATTACK: THE SOUTHERN THRUST

OBJECTIVE: A tour looking at how the German counter-attack through Mortain and the surrounding high ground, particularly Hill 317, was met and defeated by Collins' VII Corps, 7–12 August.

DURATION/SUITABILITY: A half-day tour (by car with some walking) that can swallow up a day for *aficionados*, but may be difficult in places for the disabled.

Looking north on the D977 towards the bridge over the disused railway cutting which is just beyond the petrol station. This was the centre of the Abbaye Blanche roadblock position in August 1944. *(Author)*

APPROACH TO BATTLE: Colonel Hammond D. Birks' 120th Infantry Regiment moved into Mortain from Tessy-sur-Vire on the evening of 5 August, relieving 1st Infantry Division's 18th Infantry Regiment. 120th Infantry Regiment consisted of three battalions with the following units attached: 230th Field Artillery Battalion; C/105th Engineer Battalion; and A/823rd Tank Destroyer Battalion, with a reconnaissance platoon attached. When Birks himself arrived in the early evening, 'the town was

"wide open" with business being transacted and the hotels full'. There was no sense of the Germans' impending counter-attack; for the advance elements of Birks' command it seemed that there would be excellent opportunities for a 'little rest and relaxation'.

Birks followed the outgoing regimental commander's advice and placed 2/120th Infantry, commanded by Lt Col Hardaway, on Hill 317 immediately to the west of the town and 1/120th Infantry (Lt Col William S. Bradford) on Hill 285 above Roche Grise, 2 km across the valley to the north-west, commanding the northern routes out of Mortain. Lt Col Paul McCollum's 3/120th Infantry, less K Company, was placed in reserve on the high ground west of Mortain near the regimental command post. The relief was completed by the evening of 6 August. The Germans were known to be in strength north-east of Mortain and this seemed the most likely direction of any attack. Birks ordered Hardaway to position roadblocks on all approaches to Hill 317 and attached two platoons of A/823rd Tank Destroyer Battalion to 2/120th Infantry. One tank destroyer platoon was deployed with the platoon group responsible for the Abbaye Blanche roadblock on the northern approach to the town, while the other was held in reserve in Mortain itself.

On 6 August, 3/120th Infantry was directed to proceed to Barenton and relieve Task Force X of CC B, 3rd Armored Division. This took away the regiment's reserve and left a potential gap in the southern flank around Mortain. Birks positioned C/120th Infantry near his command post to cover this flank. It appears that, while precautions were taken and that strong positions were occupied, no real threat was expected. Hardaway positioned the bulk of 2/120th Infantry on Hill 317 but located his headquarters in l'Hôtel de la Poste in the centre of town. It does not seem likely that he personally checked the battalion locations. There was very much a sense that 2/120th Infantry's time in Mortain would be easy and a just reward for all of their hard fighting to date.

Stand E1: The Abbaye Blanche Roadblock

DIRECTIONS: Drive to St-Barthélemy from Avranches on the D5, as in Tour D. After going through St-Barthélemy the D5 then links with the D977. After 2 km, you pass over a disused railway, crossing into le Neufbourg, and then, after passing a petrol station, reach a small square with an enclosed garden in front of l'Hôtel de l'Abbaye; park here.

THE ACTION: On 6 August, Lt Tom F.H. Andrew was ordered to secure and defend a roadblock at Abbaye Blanche. Andrew's platoon was augmented by Lt Tom Springfield's 1/A/823rd Tank Destroyer Battalion, equipped with four towed 3-inch anti-tank guns; a platoon of three 57-mm anti-tank guns from 120th Infantry Regiment's anti-tank company under Lt Sidney Eichler; and a mortar section and a machine-gun section from his parent company, F/120th Infantry.

> **In Birks' opinion:**
> '… if that roadblock had not held, the whole position of the 120th would have been nullified and the resulting gap would have permitted the enemy to smash through the Mortain area of the 30th Division's line. In such a "touch-and-go" battle… the consequence of a German success… might well have had disastrous implications.'
> *Source:* Combat Interview, Colonel Hammond D. Birks, 120th Infantry Regiment, USNA.

The result was a text-book defensive battle in miniature, where an infantry platoon group and supporting arms conducted a six-day resistance under intensive German armoured, infantry and air attacks, at a cost of three killed and 20 wounded. It is a rare example of a platoon-size group action that deserves tactical study for the skills shown by its commanders, Lts Springfield and Andrew.

Stand E2: The Bridge

DIRECTIONS: Walk north along the D977 to the northern side of the road bridge over the disued railway cutting. Stop at the T-junction where the side road meets the D977.

THE ACTION: The ground presented a number of problems, which Andrew had to solve with his limited force. It was better suited to a company defence but Andrew had to parcel out his infantry and anti-tank weapons to cover a series of approaches and potential axes of advance. The northern perimeter of his defence had to be placed north of the railway bridge, the securing of which was critical to north–south movement out of Mortain. Lt Springfield co-ordinated the defences in this sector.

Existing German defences sited to cover the bridge provided the

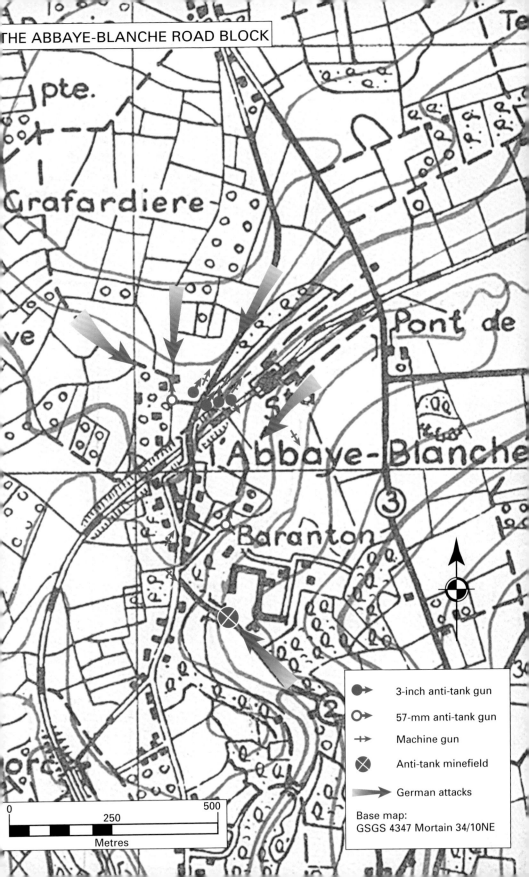

THE ABBAYE-BLANCHE ROAD BLOCK

pte.

Grafardiere

ve

Pont de

Abbaye-Blanche

Baranton

③

● →	3-inch anti-tank gun
O →	57-mm anti-tank gun
+→	Machine gun
⊗	Anti-tank minefield
➤	German attacks

Base map:
GSGS 4347 Mortain 34/10NE

0   250   500

Metres

basic structure of the defensive layout. Springfield used the four 3-inch guns and two of the 57-mm guns to cover the approaches, supported by riflemen and bazooka teams. North of the bridge and immediately north of the junction that came in sharply from the north, a 3-inch gun was placed on either side of the main road, covering the north approach, with two machine guns on each side. Springfield pushed the other two 3-inch guns forward of the rail bridge and east of the main road, one covering the main road and the other sited to cover south-east across the railway to deal with any German penetration along the road leading from the station.

Looking north along the D977 from the anti-tank positions north of the Abbaye Blanche bridge. As well as covering the approach along the road, anti-tank guns from this position covered the railway station road. *(Author)*

Forward of the bridge on the west, a bazooka and BAR team and a half-squad of riflemen were placed in a former German defensive post, by a hedgerow where the parallel north road linked up with the main road at the sharp turn. This approach was covered by a 57-mm gun, sited to fire up this road and also a minor road that curved down and linked with it from higher ground to the north-west. South of the rail bridge, riflemen and bazooka teams were dug in on either side of the road covering the northern approach. The sheer drop to the east from the road allowed Springfield to cover the river flats to the north-east; the anti-tank guns on this flank successfully engaged and destroyed vehicles attempting to by-pass the roadblock along the D246 at la Vacherie.

The first contact came at 0500 hours on 7 August, when two

half-tracks approached from the north. The first, mounting a 75-mm gun, was knocked out by Sergeant Rhyne's 57-mm gun team; the second, loaded with ammunition, was also hit and blew up. Throughout the day, Springfield's position came under constant German artillery fire and also air attack from both the *Luftwaffe* and British rocket-firing Typhoons, which wounded two 3-inch gun crewmen. German armour tried to rush the northern approach but the 3-inch guns knocked out at least 12 vehicles, possibly more. An infantry probe in mid-afternoon on 8 August involved flame-throwers and grenades; four anti-tank gun crew-members were wounded, but the attackers were wiped out by machine-gun fire.

On 8 August a German half-track drove right up to the obstacle to investigate the minefield straddling the road. Seemingly unaware that he was being watched, an NCO got out to inspect the minefield: BAR fire mowed him down and a bazooka destroyed the half-track.

Stand E3: The Square

DIRECTIONS: Walk back across the bridge down the D977 into the small square in front of the hotel.

THE ACTION: The west of the D977, looking south from the square towards Mortain, was covered by a rifle squad and two .30-calibre machine guns in a walled orchard. These overlooked the river but more importantly covered the north–south road, the junction in the square and the road leading out of the square onto the higher ground where most of the village of le Neufbourg was located. A further six men and a .50-calibre machine gun from the tank destroyer platoon were placed in and among the line of houses that linked the orchard with the railway bridge.

It was a strong position but Andrew really needed another two platoons to cover the myriad approaches. He made do with what he had and found that his small band was supplemented by stragglers and small groups, who filtered into his position over the six days that he held the block. The first critical reinforcement was on the day of the offensive, when Lt Stewart with two squads of 2/F/120th Infantry, walked into the roadblock. Stewart had been forced out of his roadblock position further towards Mortain and had withdrawn north to Abbaye Blanche. Andrew gave him the southern perimeter facing Mortain to co-ordinate. Over the next few days others of 2/120th Infantry who had been cut off in the town trickled in, so that eventually the defenders numbered some 150 men. A large number, however, were battle exhaustion cases who took little part in the actual defence of the position.

Looking south from the Abbaye Blanche roadblock towards Mortain. In 1944 a minefield was laid across the road in the area near the white vehicle. Lt Stewart knocked out a half-track and a tank with a bazooka at this location. *(Author)*

Two belts of mines had been placed across the D977 over the main road at a defile immediately north of the impressive bulk of the Abbaye Blanche, blocking the southern approach. This activity was covered by a bazooka and BAR team. Lt Stewart knocked out one half-track and one tank with bazooka fire on this front. Surprisingly there was no attempt to infiltrate the position out of the river or from the west flank; while there was sporadic firing on this flank, where Andrew assessed his position was most vulnerable, the Germans made no real effort.

Stand E4: The Railway Station Road

DIRECTIONS: Walk north-east down the road to the station. Note how the rocky outcrops shield this approach from the main defensive position forward of the bridge. Note also the high rocky outcrop north of the imposing house (built since the war) on the right or east of the road. The railway station is sadly derelict but one can see how part of the road is open to observation and fire from the high ground north of the bridge over the railway cutting.

German vehicles destroyed by 1/A/823rd Tank Destroyer Battalion and F/120th Infantry. The Mortain-le Neufbourg railway station is in the background. *(USNA)*

THE ACTION: Andrew placed a squad of eight men and a bazooka team covering the station road and open fields to the east on the rocky outcrop north of the house. A field telephone line was laid back to the rear of the rock where the mortar squad was positioned. The road was also covered by a 57-mm gun that was sited to fire down it from the little square in front of the hotel where the memorial now stands. German attempts to move up the road were beaten off by the squad in the rock.

Andrew's group continued to repel thrusts through to 12 August, when the pressure finally eased. Birks visited the position and was surprised at the few casualties suffered by the defence. Birks also marvelled at the 40 or so vehicles that littered the roads into the position, believing it to be 'the best sight I had seen in the war'.

Stand E5: Mortain – Place des Arcades

DIRECTIONS: Drive south along the D977 into Mortain. Stop at the Place des Arcades, immediately past l'Hôtel de la Poste and opposite the church.

L'Hôtel de la Poste in the centre of Mortain. Lt Col Hardaway's headquarters was here; he and his staff were later captured when the Germans overran the town. The hotel itself was totally destroyed in the fighting that followed. *(Author)*

THE ACTION: Lt Col Eads Hardaway's 2/120th Infantry, with K/3/120th attached, was taken completely by surprise by the German offensive. German infantry infiltrated around the south of Hill 317 and by-passed the roadblock established south-east of the town. At 0125 hours on 7 August small-arms fire was heard in Mortain itself, to the east of l'Hôtel de la Poste. The sound of fighting in the town led Birks to dispatch C/120th Infantry, his regimental reserve, to counter-attack the town, link up with Hardaway's headquarters and re-establish the roadblock to the south-east. Company C was overwhelmed when it moved into the town. Its commander was killed and its platoons scattered, with elements withdrawing and establishing themselves on the high ground west of the town under First Sergeant Albert J. Ruback, while its 1st Platoon was driven east, where it fought as part of G/120th Infantry in the defence of Hill 317.

Hardaway and his staff were trapped in the town and unable to link with his battalion on the hill. Birks ordered Hardaway to rejoin his battalion but was informed a few hours later that he was cut off and in hiding, with radio batteries running low. Hardaway and the entire staff were later captured. Hardaway paid the price for not establishing an advanced command post on the hill, where his battalion was in defence. It was to mean that the epic of Hill 317 would not have its commanding officer at its centre.

The *Voie de la Liberté* marker in the Place des Arcades, Mortain. *(Author)*

Birks, too, was helpless to assist. 1/120th Infantry was holding Hill 285 and he later learnt that the Abbaye Blanche roadblock was holding on. He requested support from division and was told that 2/117th Infantry would assist. Birks committed the regimental intelligence and reconnaissance platoons to occupy Romagny, a village 2 km south-west of Mortain, but they were ambushed there and only two vehicles and a few men escaped. Nothing was left; 30th Infantry Division's southern flank was wide open and ready for exploitation by a German column which had nothing between it and Avranches – if it could pass Mortain.

Stand E6: Hill 317

DIRECTIONS: Drive south through Mortain. At the edge of town, follow the signs up the narrow Rue de la Petite Chapelle, which is on the immediate left at the junction with the Route des Aubrils. In 1944 this latter road was the undefended route by which the Germans gained entry into the town. Stop at the car park signposted at the top of the hill. Walk along the road to the east to the end of the houses. It was this route, then a dirt track but now the D487E, which was the German axis of advance in August 1944.

THE SITE: Hill 317 is a steep-sided plateau feature bisected in 1944 by a dirt road which crossed the heights from the east and then contoured down the steep slopes into the town. 2/120th Infantry's positions ran north–south along the ridge astride this road and included a number of occupied farmhouses to the north of the D487E road where you now stand. As you can see from the road, the approach from the east is over open grassy fields, bounded by stone walls and trees, an area that provided good fields of fire for the defenders. 2/120th Infantry's defensive position was among pine trees growing out of rocky ground on the heights where digging was difficult and the risk of rock splinters from artillery high.

Note that there is some confusion as to the name of the feature. The official history refers to it as Hill 317, but wartime maps show the chapel knoll as Hill 314 and 120th Infantry Regiment Combat Interview Reports refer to it as such.

The open fields lying south of the D487E offered superb fields of fire to the defenders of the Hill 317 position, helping E/120th Infantry and the other elements of 2/120th Infantry on this flank to defeat repeated German probes and attacks between 7 and 12 August. *(Author)*

THE ACTION: In Hardaway's absence, Captain Reynold C. Erickson, commanding F/120th Infantry, directed 2/120th Infantry's epic defence. With him were Lt Joe C. Reaser of K/120th Infantry, holding the northern area of the ridge, north of what is now the D487E; Captain Delmont Byrn of H/120th, holding the southern perimeter with G/120th; and Lt Ralph A. Kerley of E/120th, who grouped his company with elements of F/ and H/120th to hold the eastern arc facing any attack along the axis of the D487E. Most critically of all, Erickson had two artillery observers on the position, Lts Charles A. Bartz and Robert L. Weiss of 230th Field Artillery Battalion. Their ability to bring in observed fire would be essential to 2/120th Infantry's success in repelling eight successive attacks, 7–12 August.

Throughout 7 August Hill 317 was under constant German artillery and air attack, directed by a Fieseler Storch aircraft overhead. The critical shortages were of radio batteries, medical supplies, ammunition and food, in that order; requests for these vital supplies were sent to Birks' headquarters, but for the present the defenders could but fight off each attack as it came.

On the evening of 9 August 2/120th Infantry received an ultimatum to surrender. It was delivered by a *Waffen-SS* officer,

The memorial to 30th Infantry Division on the crest of the ridge of Hill 317. *(Author)*

who approached Company E's position under a flag of truce. He spoke to Lt Elmer G. Rohmiller of Company E and Sergeant Wingate of Company G, stating that he was offering the Americans on the hill honourable surrender. He added that they were entirely surrounded, that many of their comrades were prisoners and that their position was hopeless. If they did not surrender before 2200 hours the Germans would 'blow them to bits'. Kerley refused on the spot and told the *Waffen-SS* officer that his men would not surrender as long as they had ammunition to kill Germans or a bayonet to stick into 'a Boche belly'. Wounded men added to the chorus by calling out, 'No! No! Don't surrender!' That night, armour attacked Company E's positions, spraying the defences with machine-gun fire as they advanced. The defenders could hear the attackers shouting 'Surrender! Surrender!' but beat them off.

The following day C-47s, escorted by fighters, dropped food supplies. Half of these fell outside the perimeter; patrols went out that night and brought in what they could find, which was enough to issue each man with two K-rations. Food was scavenged and some caged rabbits stolen from the French families caught inside the perimeter. The critical shortage was of medical supplies. There were no doctors and the corpsmen performed 'miracles' with what little they had. On 10 August friendly artillery used shells developed for delivering propaganda material to fire medical supplies on to the position. None of the blood plasma arrived intact but bandage, tape and morphine survived the experiment to be used.

The Germans failed to co-ordinate an effective attack, despite using artillery, tanks, armoured cars, flame-throwers, mortars, *Nebelwerfers* and everything else they had in their arsenal, and the 370-strong garrison held on until relieved on 12 August. The failure to seize Hill 317 and the bottleneck caused by the successful Abbaye Blanche roadblock were the two critical ground factors in denying the Germans the opportunity to threaten Avranches.

Stand E7: La Petite Chapelle-St-Michel

DIRECTIONS: From the D487E walk south into the park along the crest line path. This was the heart of the position, covering both the approach from the east and up steep slopes from the direction of the town to the west. A memorial commemorating 30th Infantry Division's achievements in the battle for Mortain is sited off the crest in a small clearing immediately before the chapel heights.

Climb up to the plane table and view the surrounding ground. To the south-west, the D977 runs in the direction of St-Hilaire-du-Harcouët. The importance of the heights immediately becomes obvious. North of the highway, beyond the factory complexes, one can make out Romagny and can then follow the high ground across the valley to the heights of Hill 285.

La Petite Chapelle-St-Michel. A plane table beyond overlooks the roads south-west to the coast and highlights the tactical significance of the feature. *(Author)*

THE ACTION: The Germans had surprised the town and held the valley floors, but the roadblock at Abbaye Blanche acted like a cork, preventing an effective link-up between the two German axes. As long as Hill 317 was in American hands, a further large-scale German advance beyond Mortain was impossible.

Initially, the major threat was from the pinnacle at the southern end of the ridge where la Petite Chapelle-St-Michel stands. This was captured by German infantry, infiltrating up the rocky slopes from the D487 below, during the initial attack on the night of 6/7 August. The Germans were driven off but the chapel itself became no-man's-land, with the American defensive line anchored among a series of rocky boulders barely 30 metres from the rocky rise.

Stand E8: Les Closeaux Crossroads

DIRECTIONS: Return down the hill and turn left on to the D977. Continue along the D977 for 3 km to the crossroads where the D977 meets the D46 from Romagny. On the south of the road is a *la Contre-Attaque* signpost.

French civilians of St-Sauveur-Lendelin ecstatically greet members of Leclerc's 2nd French Armoured Division as they pass south down the roads of Normandy on their way to fight, 2 August. *(USNA)*

THE ACTION: At this junction, on the afternoon of 7 August, a detachment of Maj Gen Jacques Phillippe Leclerc's 2nd French Armoured Division, a 'disparate bunch' consisting of Moroccan Spahis, a platoon of 1st Infantry Regiment and a squadron of 12th Chasseurs d'Afrique Regiment had a brush with the forward elements of 2nd SS Panzer Division's 3rd SS Panzergrenadier Regiment *Deutschland*. A jeep, driven by a junior French officer accompanied by two men, stopped at a nearby farmhouse to ask for the whereabouts of the 'Boches'. Here they were surprised and captured by the enemy they were seeking. However, Lt Nouveau of 12th Chasseurs d'Afrique took the SS men prisoner in turn and rescued the party. This minor action was the first engagement by Leclerc's Free French on the soil of France.

THIS IS THE END OF THE TOUR: To return direct to Avranches continue south-west on the D977 and then join the N176 at St-Hilaire-du-Harcouët. Tourers may instead wish to visit the American Military Cemetery at St-James. To do so

continue south on the D177 from St-Hilaire to Louvigne-du-Désert and then west on the D14 to St-James.

Originally established as a temporary cemetery soon after 8th Infantry Division liberated the area on 2 August 1944, this became one of 14 permanent overseas sites after the war. Most of the 4,410 American servicemen buried here were casualties from the break-out battles from St-Lô south to Avranches, the fighting during the Mortain counter-attack and the liberation of Brittany. It is an appropriate place to contemplate the effort, cost and success achieved by American forces in this decisive battle.

To conclude the tour drive north from St-James on the D998 to Avranches.

'Here rests in honoured glory a Comrade in Arms known but to God'. One of 95 headstones marking the graves of unknown soldiers in the St-James cemetery. The cemetery also hold the remains of 20 pairs of brothers who now rest side by side. (*Author*)

BATTLEFIELD TOURS

PART FOUR

ON YOUR
RETURN

FURTHER RESEARCH

As you will have found out on the tours, this book by its nature can only scratch the surface of the many actions and stories that are part of the rich tapestry of Operation Cobra, the break-out into Brittany and Operation *Lüttich*, the German attempted counter-offensive. If you wish to delve further into these operations and into the Battle of Normandy as a whole then below is a list of additional reading, primary source archives and museums that may prove of interest. Obviously a very useful source of information for all aspects of the Normandy campaign are the other volumes in the 'Battle Zone Normandy' series.

There is a growing library of books on Operation Cobra and the Mortain counter-attack. The best place to begin in terms of accessible secondary sources is James Jay Carafano's *After D-Day: Operation Cobra and the Normandy Breakout* (Boulder, Colorado, 2000) which is both detailed and unusually critical of General Collins. I enjoyed arguing against it as I walked the ground. Mark J. Reardon's *Victory at Mortain: Stopping Hitler's Panzer Counteroffensive* (Lawrence, Kansas, 2002) is also superbly researched and a pleasure to read, as is Alwyn Featherston's *Saving the Breakout: The 30th Division's Heroic Stand at Mortain, August 7–12, 1944* (Novato, California, 1993). These are backed by Steven J. Zaloga's *Operation Cobra 1944: Breakout from Normandy* (Oxford, 2001) which is brief and incisive as are all of Zaloga's many studies on US armoured doctrine and the organisation and tactical employment of US armoured divisions and tank and tank destroyer units in the European theatre. Central to any study is Martin Blumenson's substantial volume in the United States Official History World War Two series. *Breakout and Pursuit* (Washington, 1961) may be daunting in terms of size but is thoroughly enjoyable for its narrative grasp and the insight that Blumenson offers on the evolving plan, course of the campaign, events and personalities, backed by excellent maps. My assessment of tactical doctrine was underpinned by Michael D. Doubler's *Closing with the Enemy: How GIs fought the war in Europe 1944–1945* (Lawrence, 1994).

Above: The memorial on the church wall in le Mesnil-Durand; 119th Infantry Regiment began its attack on 25 July from near here. *(Author)*

Page 185: A medical jeep passes a column of Sherman tanks, near St-Lô, 25 July. *(USNA)*

One has to read about the principal players and I recommend General Collins' autobiography, *Lightning Joe* (Novato, California, 1994); Omar Bradley's *A Soldier's Story* (New York, 1951); David Eisenhower's biography of his grandfather, *Eisenhower at War 1943–1945* (New York, 1991); Carlo D'Este, *A Genius for War: A Life of General George S. Patton* (London, 1995); and also his *Decision in Normandy* (London, 1984) which with Max Hasting's *Overlord*, (London, 1984) are two easily accessible general histories of the Battle of Normandy that also offer valuable insights into Cobra and *Lüttich*. The importance of tactical air power to the ground operations is covered in Thomas A. Hughes' *Overlord: General Pete Quesada and the Triumph of Tactical Air Power in World War II* (New York, 1995) and a fascinating chronological study of the later stages can be found in Robert A. Miller's *August 1944: The Campaign for France* (Novato, California, 1988).

On the other side of the hill, I enjoyed Samuel W. Mitcham, Jnr's *Retreat to the Reich: The German Defeat in France, 1944* (Westport, Connecticut, 2000) and, although its lack of indexing can be an exercise in frustration, the wartime intelligence debriefs of the principal German generals in *Fighting the Breakout: The German Army in Normandy from 'Cobra' to the Falaise Gap* (London, 2004), edited by David C. Isby. An interesting pictorial history of the Normandy campaign that has not been translated but has invaluable images, both common and many not normally seen, is Eric Rondel, *Les Américains en Normandie – Été 1944* (Sables d'Or, les Pins, 2004).

In terms of primary source archive material the US National Archives at College Park on the outskirts of Washington, DC, contain a vast repository of documents relating to US military operations in Normandy as well as copies of large numbers of translated German documents, and a treasure trove of photos and maps. Here one can sift through individual war diaries from army group to battalion, and access thousands of personal accounts of the fighting in the combat interviews. I have not mentioned the large number of published divisional and unit accounts, which are backed by the many regimental/unit associations whose contact details can be established on the internet. The websites of the US Library of Congress, the US National Archives and the Military History Institute are invaluable. The internet is also a very worthwhile source of a tremendous amount of ephemera connected to the Second World War in general, and specific engagements and units in particular.

In Britain the obvious starting points for research are the National Archives at Kew and the Imperial War Museum. In the UK another interesting site connected with the Normandy fighting is the American Cemetery at Madingley in Cambridgeshire. This impressive and emotive location holds the remains of 3,812 US military personnel killed on active service in the European theatre and also has a memorial to 5,162 who have no known grave.

Useful Addresses

Imperial War Museum, Lambeth Road, London SE1 6HZ; tel: 020 7416 5320; email: <mail@iwm.org.uk>; web: <www.iwm.org.uk>.

UK National Archives, Public Record Office, Kew, Richmond, Surrey TW9 4DU; tel: 020 8876 3444; email: <enquiry@nationalarchives.gov.uk>; web: <www.nationalarchives.gov.uk>.

US National Archives, The National Archives and Records Administration, 8601 Adelphi Road, College Park, MD 20740–6001; tel: +01 866 272 6272; web: <www.archives.gov>.

Madingley American Military Cemetery, Coton, Cambridge CB3 7PH; tel: 01954 210350; web: <www.abmc.gov>. Cambridge American Cemetery and Memorial is located 5 km west of Cambridge on the A1303. Open 0900–1700 daily, except 25 Dec & 1 Jan.

INDEX

Page numbers in *italics* denote
an illustration.

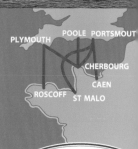